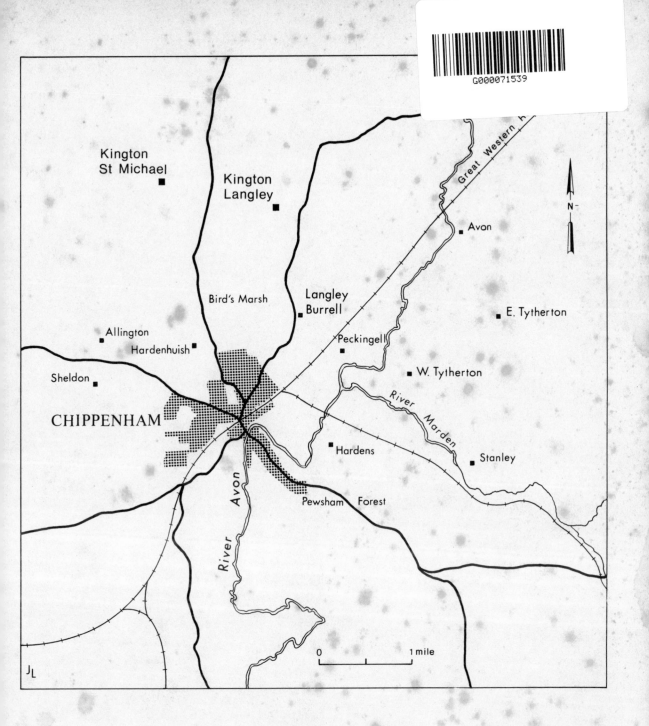

Kington
St Michael

Kington
Langley

Avon

Bird's Marsh

Langley
Burrell

E. Tytherton

Allington

Peckingell

Hardenhuish

W. Tytherton

Sheldon

River Marden

CHIPPENHAM

Hardens

Stanley

River Avon

Pewsham Forest

Great Western

N

0   1 mile

J L

Greater Chippenham area

COCKLEBURY:

A Farming Area and its People
in the Vale of Wiltshire

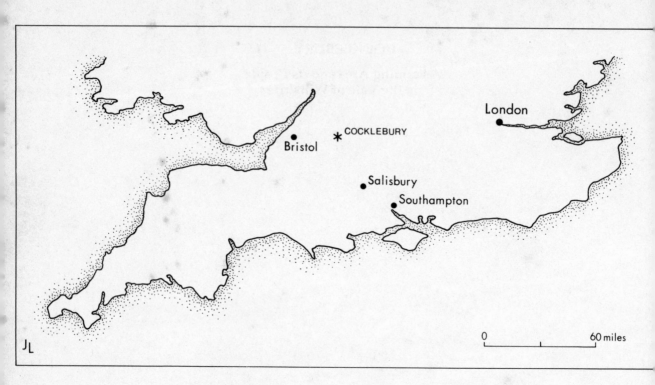

Bristol

✳ COCKLEBURY

London

Salisbury

Southampton

0   60 miles

JL

Southern England

COCKLEBURY

**A farming area and its people
in the Vale of Wiltshire**

Avice R. Wilson

Maps by Janice Limb
Drawings by Tobie Wallis and Henry Pedersen

Phillimore

1983

published by
PHILLIMORE & CO. LTD.
Shopwyke Hall, Chichester, Sussex

ISBN 0 85033 510 8

Printed and bound in Great Britain by
THE CAMELOT PRESS
Southampton, England

To Peggy, who began the story for me,
and to her niece, Serena Self,
with the hope that she will one day
farm at Cocklebury and so continue
the story for everyone

Contents

List of Illustrations

(between pages 44 and 45)

List of Maps

Foreword

As the reader turns each page so the evolution of Cocklebury unfolds. Some would say how tragic that such an unspoilt corner of this beautiful county should be transformed into bricks and mortar, others, particularly those living there, would express their good fortune at finding themselves in such a lovely area and perhaps not even consider the matter further.

But what has happened at Cocklebury is happening all around us, particularly in the West of England. There is a strong natural tide of inward migration from the turbulence of our cities into the relative security and tranquility of our smaller towns and villages.

Each field lost to development when multiplied across the country adds up to a staggering erosion of agricultural land each year. The rate and extent of these developments is not fully known, that is the danger. It would be naive and unrealistic to imagine this movement of population could be completely halted. In a free country why should not people live where they want?

However, there is a real risk that the very reason which motivates people to move, the search for a better quality of life, will evaporate under the sheer weight of numbers. Ending up with everyone being the losers, those who have moved and those who were there before.

To avoid this needs a change of policy. Sensible policies can only be determined when all the facts are known. At present they are not. We neither know the rate or extent of land being developed nor, and perhaps as important, the loss of agricultural land at the interface between town and country.

Roads, factories and houses often create a 'no man's land' where the two meet. Normal farming becomes impossible resulting in, at the worst, dereliction and, at the best, that new industry of equiculture! The only way to avert today's mistakes which tomorrow's generations will live to regret is through greater knowledge.

We need to measure the loss of land on a regular basis. This can only be done by detailed land surveys. There have been three national utilisation surveys over the past millennium. The Domesday in 1086, Sir Dudley Stamp's in the thirties and Miss Coleman's in the sixties. Only when we know what is happening round about us will there be a change of enlightened decisions altering the present pattern of growth.

Mrs. Avice Wilson's objective and enjoyable study of Cocklebury should help to focus our attention on not only the individual case but the county as a whole.

Bowood House
Calne
Wiltshire

Shelburne. July 1983.

Preface

This is the story of what has happened to 400 acres (162 hectares) of land in north-west Wiltshire, from its geological formation to the mixture of farmland, industrial complex, and urban sprawl it is today. The search for information about Cocklebury has resembled the solving of a jig-saw puzzle. Some pieces were easily found and put together; others proved elusive and had to be deduced; a few will never be discovered. Assembled and fitted together, however, despite some gaps, the individual pieces emerge as an entirety. Essentially it is a local history; woven into its fabric are geological, archaeological, economic and agrarian details.

My life-long association with Cocklebury has helped me to tell its story, and I was greatly assisted by the writings of W. G. Hoskins. His pioneer studies of land history, particularly his book *The Making of the English Landscape*, originally set me on the trail of this story, and provided me with the basic concepts to understand the continuity of forces that have shaped the area.

Cocklebury offers a microcosm of English history. Nomadic Stone Age peoples passed along the river valley; Iron Age people settled there; the Romans apparently ignored it, although the British knew it; Saxons cleared its woodland, and husbanded the resulting fields. By Norman times, competition had begun for its agricultural riches, culminating by the reign of Henry VIII in monastic ownership of two-thirds of its land, ownership that was transferred by a single stroke of the pen to Henry's brother-in-law, Edward Seymour. He and his descendants became absentee landlords. Three centuries and many documents later, Cocklebury was in the possession of two families, and so remained until the 20th century.

The first intrusion into Cocklebury came in 1840. The Great Western Railway Company cut its main line from London to Bristol, and later, another line was built from Chippenham to Calne. These slashed the area into three sections. One section formed the nucleus of what was to become the most important industrial complex in Chippenham. Another became in the 1960s the town's largest housing estate. On the third section, another industrial estate is being built. It is likely that the demands of today's society will obliterate the farmland remaining in this section of Cocklebury before another generation has passed.

The disappearance of so many acres of attractive countryside, which is also prime food-producing land, is a common occurrence today. Such losses will continue until the demands of a growth society are halted, either by choice or because it will become too expensive to create growth. Before the days of imported food, the needs of the land were put before the wants of the people, for, as this story shows, the food the land produced was essential for survival. In the past two centuries this concept has been reversed. Now it is time to change again, to care for and to nurture the soil on which man's survival ultimately depends. To eliminate the farm is to destroy society.

As the story progressed, it became apparent to me that land serves man. In return, man must serve the land, or he perishes.

Author's Notes

In quotations of old deeds, legal documents and other manuscripts, punctuation has been supplied to ensure meaning. I make no apology for the presence of dates. They are not meant to be learnt, but are included to establish sequence. No attempt has been made to adjust old-style dating. Neither do I apologise for the 'perhaps', the 'probables' and the 'no doubts' in this book. They are used to usher in the unestablished, the unknown and the uncertain.

Unless otherwise mentioned, all interpretations of facts are my own, and I am responsible for any errors.

Acknowledgements

Every person who writes a book of this scope has always to admit that all those people who were involved in its preparation are too numerous to list individually. I am in the same predicament, regretfully, for I would like to mention everyone. Hence I can only set down the names of those who gave me the most help. Some are acknowledged in the text or in the notes to the chapters. But there are others behind the scenes who spent a great deal of time on my behalf.

Amongst librarians and other guardians of books and records, Mr. Kenneth Rogers, the County Archivist at the Wiltshire Record Office, is top of the list; his exacting standards were often frightening, but his help was always at hand when needed. Other staff of the WRO were always willing to seek out documents and answer questions. Miss E. Green at the Wiltshire room of the Devizes County Library deserves a special mention, not only for carrying all those heavy volumes that make up the files of the *Devizes and Wiltshire Gazette*, but also for her suggestions for sources of information for this book. The Chippenham branch of the County Library service takes a prize for speedy production of books requested. Miss B. Austen, the Librarian at Longleat House, enabled me to dive deeply into the Seymour papers concerning Monkton. The late Mr. R. M. Sandell at the Wiltshire Archaeological Society's Library at Devizes never found any of my problems too much trouble to solve.

In the United States, I wish to thank Mr. Leslie Ota and other Librarians of the Reference Section of the Alexander Library of Rutgers University, New Brunswick, New Jersey, and Mrs. H. Seitz, who located so many books and microfilm material for me from university libraries in all parts of the U.S.A. My acknowledgements go also to the Firestone Library of Princeton University for their exceptionally complete collection of books on Wiltshire.

I wish to thank Derrick Hale for permission to reproduce the watercolour used as the jacket illustration.

I should also like to thank the Self family for providing so many photographs, and The Earl of Shelburne for his kindness in providing a Foreword.

To my family and friends, and all those who have shown so much interest in this book for so long, I thank you for your encouragement.

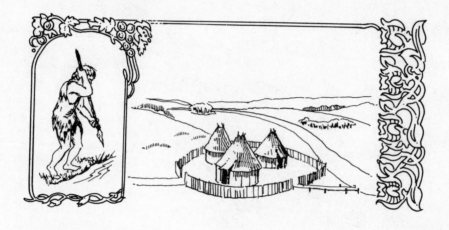

Chapter One

The Beginning of the Story

In southern England there is a narrow pastoral valley known as the Wiltshire Vale. It curves gently from north to south in the form of a crescent, and through most of its length the Bristol Avon flows serenely. Spaced along the river are bustling towns, the centres of many different industries. Away from these towns, villages and hedge-lined fields cover the floor of the valley, creating a patchwork pattern as far as the eye can see. In the west, the valley is fringed by the southern edge of the Cotswold hills; to the east it reaches upwards to a wooded sandy ridge in front of the Wiltshire Chalklands.

Right in the middle of the Vale lies Cocklebury, an area of 400 acres, enclosed in a bend of the Avon immediately north of Chippenham. For 1000 years and more the land at Cocklebury was used by man to produce food; first for his own sustenance; later, as markets and better ways of farming developed, to feed others. During the past 150 years the growth of Chippenham has required space. So, piece by piece, Cocklebury has been taken from farming in order to fulfill a variety of needs.

In the beginning, these encroachments were gradual: a few houses before 1840; two railways and several small factories with homes nearby for their workers by 1900; more dwellings and the expansion of industrial facilities by 1960–a total of 100 acres lost. But in the last 20 years, more than 120 acres have been built over, and an expanding industrial estate is now threatening the existence of the remaining farm at Cocklebury.

1

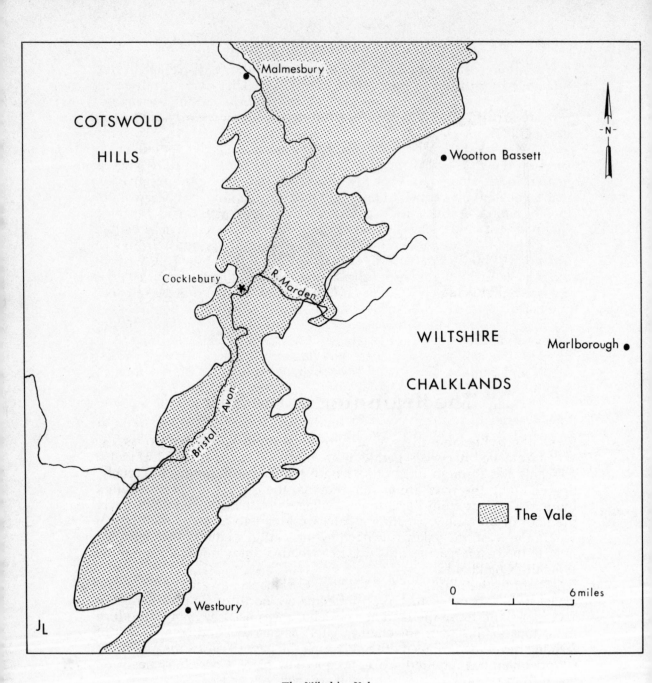

COTSWOLD

HILLS

Malmesbury

-N-

Wootton Bassett

Cocklebury   R. Marden

WILTSHIRE

CHALKLANDS

Marlborough

Bristol Avon

The Vale

0   6 miles

Westbury

JL

The Wiltshire Vale

It is here, around Rawlings farmhouse, that the fields still retain their original pattern from medieval and Tudor days. They slope gently to the river, their colours and textures varying through the farming seasons, to provide an attractive corner of the fast-disappearing countryside around Chippenham.

The story of Cocklebury is a story of change; change over millions of years as the rock layers now far below its soils were formed; change as natural forces shaped an evolving valley; and recently, change caused by man's constant alterations to the natural landscape. The story begins with the formation of the surface rocks that are now present in the area. Composed of sands, clays and limestones, they lie to a depth of more than 300 metres on older rocks whose formations and structures are as yet unknown. These surface rocks at Cocklebury were formed in a period roughly 300-100 million years ago. During this time many climatic changes occurred, producing cycles of dry and wet periods. In dry times, salt lakes and deserts formed, while in wet periods, heavy rains would produce great expanses of water often to remain on the land for a long time, creating sediments at the bottom of these lakes or seas. Each time a sea dried up or receded, the sediments remained, building up a series of layers of varying depth and content. Eventually the weight of the layers caused them to compress and to form horizontal beds of differing rocks.

Through exposure to the elements, these rocks began to wear away. In time a series of levels evolved in the region, the Vale being the lowest, surrounded by rocks that are now known as the Cotswold hills, the Somerset Mendips and the Wiltshire Chalklands. It is these levels that make up the basic topography of the area and on which its first landscape was formed.

The valley itself was created by the erosion of a deep bed of clay which had formed there over many millions of years. Due to the impermeability of clay and its slippery qualities when wet, it wore away much faster than its surrounding rocks. As the clay bed lowered, a watercourse and its tributaries became established on it and further hastened erosion. Periodically, climate changes would melt accumulated snows and ice. Then from the surrounding higher areas, torrential sheets of water would sweep over the forming valley. These floods carried flints and stone from as far away as the Chalklands, and the large deposits of gravels lying along the Avon at Cocklebury and other parts of the Vale are evidence of these long-ago actions.

The underlying rocks at Cocklebury today have been named the Kellaways Clay, the Kellaways Sands, the Cornbrash, and the Forest Marble. The Kellaways Sands are the remains of a sandbank formed at the edge of an open sea and never totally eroded away to the underlying clay. The Cornbrash and the small section of the Forest Marble in the southwest corner of Cocklebury are two of the limestone strata that make up the Great Oolite Series, which produces the famous Bath building stone.

At the end of the last Ice Age in Britain (approximately 100,000 to 14,000 bp), the snows melted to reveal the clay valley as being much the configuration that it is today, whilst its river had assumed practically the same course its meanderings take at present. However, it was bare of any vegetation and its rocks were exposed. These rocks are very important to the subsequent history of the Vale and to the story of Cocklebury, for their presence decided the nature and the drainage of the soils that were to form above them. In turn, the soils, in conjunction with the prevailing climate, would determine the natural cover of the landscape, and later the crops man would grow in them.

At first, when soil accumulation began, the prevailing cold climate only allowed such vegetation as lichen and mosses to gain a foothold, forming a tundra-like surface. After several thousand years the climate became milder (somewhat similar to Sweden today), and such trees as larch, birch, hazel and pine began to grow on the accumulated humus. Later, more warmth enabled elm, lime and alder to grow in the valley. By 4,000 bp the oak tree had appeared, to become in time the chief cover of the area–including, of course, Cocklebury. But in Cocklebury, one section of the land, along the river and in the southwest corner above the limestones, was to remain more open.

It was these clearer areas, more easily travelled than woodland, that attracted man to Cocklebury 10,000 years or so ago, to hunt and to fish, to use as part of a route to cross the wooded valley, and later, to create temporary settlements by the river and above the Cornbrash.

The earliest trace of man so far found near Cocklebury is an early Palaeolithic hand axe, c.250,000 bp. It was discovered in a gravel bed four miles north of Cocklebury. The axe showed no evidence of being carried by water from a far-away area, as it was quite unworn. This suggests that it was discarded by its owner at or near its final resting place.

Long after this hand axe had been dropped, glacial periods continued, and such climatic conditions apparently kept man away from the valley, for very few other Palaeolithic tools have been found, and none as old as this axe is reputed to be. It is not until c.12,000-10,000 bp that the next indication occurs of man using the valley, and this time he came to Cocklebury.

The earliest traces of prehistoric man actually found at Cocklebury are an Upper Palaeolithic blade tool found in a gravel bed of the Avon near the site of Black Bridge, plus a number of Mesolithic tools discovered above the Cornbrash on a ridge 60 feet from the river. The craftsmanship of the Mesolithic tools shows them to be the work of a single human group, probably a wandering band of food-gathering hunters living in the middle of the Mesolithic period, c.10,000-6,000 bp. Made from flints present in nearby gravels by the river, the tools consist of small blades, scrapers, and flakes left over from trimming. The original flint cores were also present, indicating that all the tools were knapped at Cocklebury for immediate use. Their abandonment is typical of a short-stay camp site, where tools were

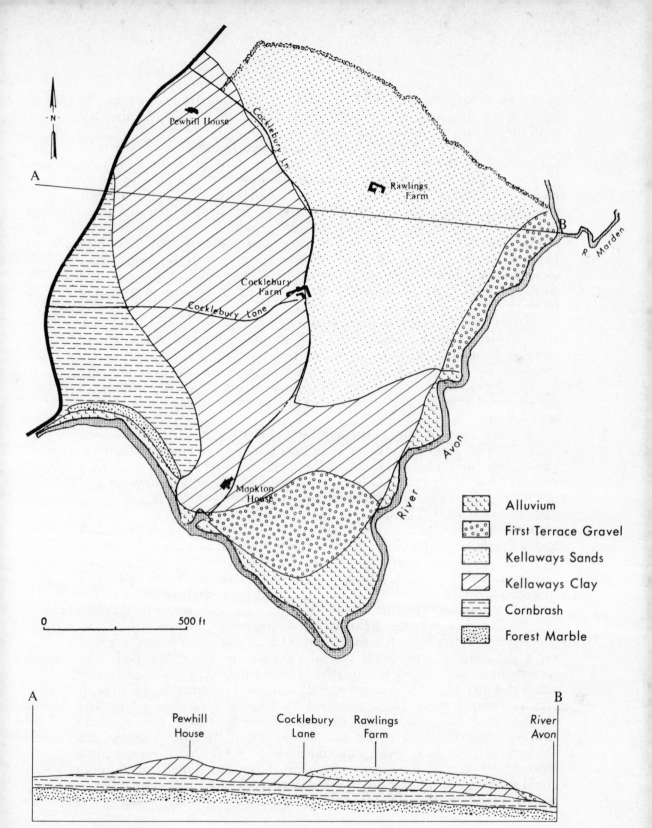

Pewhill House

Cocklebury Ln.

Rawlings Farm

R. Marden

Cocklebury Farm

Cocklebury Lane

River Avon

Monkton House

	Alluvium
	First Terrace Gravel
	Kellaways Sands
	Kellaways Clay
	Cornbrash
	Forest Marble

0   500 ft

A

Pewhill
House

Cocklebury
Lane

Rawlings
Farm

River
Avon

B

J L

Geology of Cocklebury

produced as required, and the by-products of the industry left behind. On this occasion they gradually became overlaid with soil, to remain unheeded until their discovery some 8,000 years later.

Similar tools of the same period have been found at another site at Cocklebury, in the north-west corner near the division of the Kellaways Clay and Sands. The particular shapes of all these tools, along with others found at Allington, two miles west of Cocklebury, indicates that their creators were apparently strongly influenced by people of three other cultures who were known to have been present in southern England during Mesolithic times.[1] Their existence also suggests that the Chippenham area was a meeting place of these cultures with the Avon valley serving as a connecting route between the higher lands to the east and west, and the Thames valley in the north. Cocklebury was, so to speak, on the map 8,000 years ago.

Two thousand years later, small tribes which had begun the domestication of plants and animals, moved into southern England and began to establish temporary–and later permanent–agricultural sites on light, easily-cultivated soils. Although no traces of such settlements have been found at Cocklebury, aerial photographs of the Vale taken during the dry summer of 1976 showed shadow-sites on the river gravels at the village of Avon just north of the area.

Confirmation of later settlement at Cocklebury has, however, been made. Several years ago a cache of animal bones were found in the river bank; after careful examination, these were considered to be part of a rubbish heap of an Iron Age village c.2,500 bp. The bones, unworn and obviously deposited at the site, were representative of oxen, pig and sheep, domestic animals that evidently played an important part in the economy of the settlement. Other bones included those of wild animals, beaver, wolf and red deer, no doubt the remains from the spoils of hunting. In addition, two horse teeth were found, but it was not possible to determine whether they belonged to either a wild or a domesticated animal. Signs of known human activity consisted of cut bones, including a sawn segment of the antler of a red deer. The cutting pattern at the end of the segment indicates that the saw was of metal, a clue to the dating of the settlement.

What form might such a settlement at Cocklebury have taken? Located on a flat marshy area (until recently known as the Withy Bed), the settlement is likely to have consisted of a few huts on piles or platforms above the marshy ground, constructed with reeds growing by the river. It was a convenient site, for it provided food easily obtainable by hunting small animals from the woods, duck and other fowl from marshy lands nearby, while fish and eels could be caught in the river. Behind the settlement, the higher, dryer, slope on the edge of the woodland would be cleared and planted for cereal cultivation. From the settlement, hunters could easily move up and down the clearer river banks for many miles in search of food, another advantage to its position. And, being on one of the ancient routes used to traverse the Vale, the location provided the opportunity to encounter other people who were travelling for trading purposes or seeking new settlement areas.

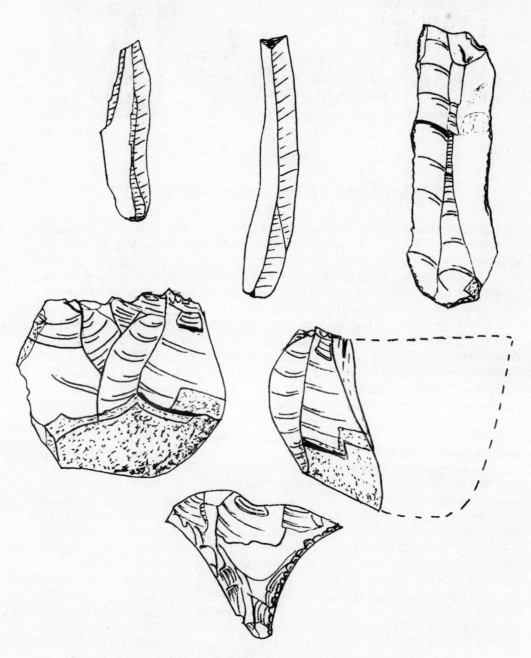

An assortment of Mesolithic and Neolithic tools found in the Cocklebury area

Chapter Two

Saxon Conquest and Settlement

Very little change took place at Cocklebury during the six centuries following the creation of the Iron Age community discussed in the last chapter. Similar agricultural settlements probably continued to be developed near the banks of the River Avon, but the woodland at Cocklebury is likely to have remained untouched through the four centuries of Roman occupation of the countryside until the coming of the Saxons.[1]

The Romans invaded Britain in 53 AD and their arrival resulted in considerable activity in and around the Vale. The towns of Bath and Cirencester were founded; iron ore was extracted at Sandy Lane (which the Romans called Verluccio); a road was built across the Vale; and several villa complexes were established. There are few, if any, surviving Roman place names on the clay soil areas of the Vale, and except for a brick kiln constructed at Minety, it seems that the Romans and the native population under their influence avoided this area. So perhaps it can be said that if any Roman saw Cocklebury, it was through the eyes of a traveller, and one far away from his usual route.

By the fourth century, the Romans had abandoned the Vale, leaving its people to their own devices. Their way of life for a time was no doubt still influenced by Roman customs, but as generation succeeded generation, this influence waned, and the British (or Celts as they have often been called) established their own social and cultural patterns. They became highly individualistic farmers who shunned political activity and remained in small family or tribal units. Settlements belonging to this period have recently been found at Allington, and such settlements are likely to have existed at Cocklebury, the lands above the Cornbrash being used for arable crops, the riverside grasslands for grazing cattle, and the woodlands for 'pannage' (pig grazing).

Towards the end of the fifth century, after the Romans had withdrawn from Britain, bands of invaders from Europe–later to be known as Saxons–began to penetrate southern England. In time, they reached areas around the Vale. It seems that at first the British were able to repel them successfully. Led by a man legend calls King Arthur, the British emerged victorious at the battle of Mount Badon, about 500 AD. The actual site of this battle is still undiscovered, but there is some evidence that it should be identified as a hill near Bath. In time, however, the Saxons began to win over the British and their final victory in 577 AD–probably at Dyrham, 10 miles west of Cocklebury–gave them control of all the area from the River Severn to the Wiltshire chalklands.

It was once assumed that all the beaten British fled after the victorious battle at Dyrham, to settle farther west in such areas as Cornwall and Wales. However, many must have remained, as local skirmishes occurred for several decades afterwards. But the subsequent agricultural development and colonisation of the Vale points to an eventual peaceful integration of the Saxons and the British, a co-existence which was in time to produce a new culture–the English.

Apparently the Saxons showed little interest in anything Roman. They rejected Latin (although in later centuries it again became the official written language) and allowed Roman villas, cities and military roads to fall into disuse. But they could not ignore the defeated British, for despite the labour provided by their own families (who had either travelled along on campaigns or joined them after fighting), the Saxons needed them to help establish their agriculture and to consolidate their claims in a new country. And for the British, there was no way that they, as the conquered, could rid themselves of their conquerors.

A clue to the peaceful integration of the Saxons and the British in the Vale area lies in the names the British had given to natural features in the Vale when they were its only inhabitants. These names were retained through Saxon times; many of them are still in use today, and there are many more that were only superseded in the last century. Around Cocklebury, several rivers and streams bear British names. Avon is derived from the Old British word *abona* denoting river. The Biss, a tributary of the Avon, is likely to have sprung from *bissi* meaning finger, here used in the sense of a fork in the Avon. Gauze brook gave its name to Corston, near Malmesbury, *cors* being similar in sound to *gauze* which signifies reeds or bog in Welsh or Cornish. The Calne, now the River Marden, and Idover brook, now Brinkworth brook, are other tributaries of the Avon whose names are also of British origin. Another pre-Saxon natural feature name, though not connected with water, is Braydon. It was used to refer to the wooded section north of the Vale beyond Minety until the last remnants of Braydon forest were cut down in the 17th century. Today, it remains as a prefix to the place name of Bradenstoke.[2]

Most of the place-names in the Vale are Saxon, suggesting that these settlements were created by the invaders. Cocklebury is one of these Saxon place-names, and there are several possible explanations for the name's origin and meaning. The first element of Cocklebury may derive from *coccel* or *coquoil* meaning tares or weeds present in growing corn, or *cocc* indicating a bird, all from the Old English; from a personal Saxon name *Kokel*; or from the Old French via the late Latin, *coquil* and *coccus* indicating cockle.

Since the time of John Aubrey, the 17th-century writer and observer of rural life, the last origin has always been preferred, but it is not necessarily correct.[3] Bivalve fossils have been found in the Cornbrash stratum in the south-west corner of Cocklebury and perhaps in the gravels along the Avon, but most of the area lies on the Kellaways Sands and Clay, producing no fossils remotely resembling cockles. It is also unlikely that the Saxons named Cocklebury after fossils found on less than 20 per cent of its area, with a word appearing later than the second element of the name. As it does not fit the language, *Kokel* is unlikely to have been in use as a personal Saxon name. This leaves the prefix Cockle as indicating weeds or birds, both logical origins. For on such fertile land, the corn crops are likely to have included burdock and other weeds, while the presence of the river attracted numerous birds.

The second element 'bury' has two choices for its origin, both from the Old English, *beorg* or *burgh* (or *burh*). The latter can be discarded if signifying a fortified place, for it was hardly likely to be used to describe Cocklebury when such a place already existed directly across the Avon at Chippenham. This leaves *beorg*, indicating a hill, or sometimes a central area of a village. Again both origins are reasonable explanations, though the hill, gently sloping to the river at Cocklebury, may be more likely as it was in existence there before any settlement.

So a choice may be made after assembling the most likely element meanings. It may mean 'hill of birds' or 'hill where the weeds grow in the corn', but not 'hill where the cockles are found', for despite Aubrey, this is inaccurate. Whatever its origins, Cocklebury's distinctive name has survived to the 20th century as denoting an agricultural area, and will survive to the next century as denoting an industrial estate.

When Cocklebury and other Saxon settlement sites in the Vale acquired their names is difficult to determine, and as yet, little of the chronological order of settlement can be discovered from studying these place-names. It is probable that the invaders at first took the easy way of settlement by cultivating land already in use by the British and extended it until all the lighter soil areas were utilized. Then clearing of the forest cover of the Vale would be undertaken. This was not a daunting task for the Saxons, as they had suitable ploughs capable of working the heavier soils that invariably lay under the woodlands.

The chief aims of the Saxon invasion were to find new lands to settle, and from them to create new kingdoms. Nowhere is this more strongly evident than in the Vale and Wessex. The land became the kingdom, the Wessex kings held the land, and, if they did not wish to have the use of it themselves, they conveyed it by royal grant to a person or a religious establishment, to be held on the Crown's behalf. The concept of direct ownership of land did not develop until after Saxon times. Gradually the land in the Vale was divided up into portions, later known as estates. The Crown held numerous estates, and was to grant much land in the northern part of the Vale to a religious house, Malmesbury Abbey; the grants commenced in 675, and continued until the 10th century.

Before forest land could be used for the cultivation of crops, it had of course to be cleared. Control of such clearances on land to be part of the Kings' estates was apparently exercised by a member of the royal household or his local representative, and before starting, designated work points in the forest were set up. Around Cocklebury several such points may have been sites bearing the names Langley, Studley, Startley, and Stanley, for they all contain the element 'ley'. Ley is derived from 'leah' and in Anglo-Saxon indicates either a natural space or open area in the forest, or the centre of a woodland estate.

When clearing commenced at Cocklebury cannot exactly be determined, but its nearness to the major river crossing of the area, its location in the bend of the Avon, and its fine sandy loams above the Kellaways Sands and Clay strata were all advantages that would make it an area to be settled before others of less convenient locations and heavier soils.

At first the woodland may have been used by the Saxons for pannage, access for this purpose perhaps being the origin of the first track into Cocklebury. This commenced at the top of Pew Hill as it does today. For nearly a mile it followed the division of the Kellaways Sands and Clay, and then continued straight to the River Avon, opposite the site of the later fortifications of Saxon Chippenham. Along this division were to be found springs which would have assured labourers and their families of an easily-accessible water supply. Near the springs would be built dwelling places for the new settlers; huts crudely constructed of roughly-trimmed tree branches, wattle daub, and clay floors, primitive structures needing constant rebuilding. It is likely that at this time a nucleus for settlement at Cocklebury was created, a narrow strip of land midway along the track, to be known in later centuries as Cocklebury Common.

Clearance of the woodland began with slash-and-burn techniques, and sections were gradually carved out of the woods to form fields where arable crops could be grown. It probably took very little time to discover how fertile the soils were at Cocklebury, and with its riverside meadows the area would soon emerge as a most desirable estate unit, easily providing the resources needed to support its labourers, and to add to the wealth of its holder. All the land surrounding Cocklebury was held by the Crown for most of the Saxon period. Lacking evidence to the contrary, it is highly likely that the holders of Cocklebury, from its clearance until the middle of the 10th century, were the Kings of Wessex.

While Cocklebury was being fashioned into working agricultural land, Malmesbury Abbey was still the recipient of many land grants from the Kings of Wessex. The text of these grants survive, some with descriptions of their boundaries, and they indicate that settlement proceeded steadily in the Vale over the seventh and eighth centuries. By the ninth century, the area north and west of Cocklebury had been formed into a large royal estate, centred around Kington Langley and Kington St Michael. It is possible that this estate was a *villa regis*, and that Cocklebury was a unit of the estate at the time. A description of such an estate portrays it as consisting of: 'a number of smaller units, containing within their bounds all the resources necessary to maintain their economy, including arable, pasture, meadow, woodland, water and either hill or marsh grazing'.[4] This description accurately fits Cocklebury at that time, and it is quite plausible to consider it in mid-Saxon times as a unit of a *villa regis* centred a few miles away.

As the years went by and one generation of labourers succeeded another at Cocklebury, estate customs would emerge, defining how the work of the unit was to be carried out, by whom, and when. These customs were probably based on laws laid down by King Ine of Wessex and later by King Alfred.[5] In time the right of a particular family to tenure of a specific portion of land would become established, and the right would be passed on to a widow or son. This *laen* land, as it was called, could not be bought or sold by its tenants; but neither could they be displaced if, for instance, the land was granted to another holder and a change of landlord took place. Towards the end of Saxon times, the rent of such land was likely to have been paid partially by services to the estate and partially by currency. Eventually in Norman times rent would be paid by money alone. By the 12th century, there were several smallholders of land at Cocklebury paying taxes to the Sheriff of Wiltshire, and it is possible that these men were descendants of the holders of *laen* land of the 10th century.

Besides the evolution of tenants into owners at Cocklebury, another change in the pattern of landholding took place there during the 10th and 11th centuries. From later documentary evidence, it is apparent that at this time, Cocklebury was divided between two estates; the King's estate at Chippenham and a newly-formed estate at Langley, later known as Langley Burrell. Langley estate had probably emerged from a reorganisation made towards the middle of the 10th century of the royal estate centred around Kington Langley. The line dividing Cocklebury also became a parish boundary. This was an unusual occurrence in Saxon times, for such a boundary seldom bisected a named area of land such as Cocklebury already was at the time. The explanation may lie in the pressing need at the end of the 10th century for the church to assure itself of a regular income for the support of its priests, and its desire to commence building permanent houses of worship.

Christianity had spread to Wessex and was the dominant religion by the beginning of the eighth century. As it spread, a system of daughter churches controlled by a mother church had evolved, but these churches did not reach all the people, and until the 10th century, the population of the countryside was not enough to support full parish systems. The formation of parishes was also delayed by the Danish invasions and the subsequent plundering which impoverished much of the church in Wessex, and no doubt also in many parts of the Vale. Later, as the population grew, the concept of an estate having its own priest–a man of holy orders of an established religious house but employed by the estate lord–became viable. In time Langley would have had its own priest, employed by the holder of the estate, and to a certain extent under his control. Larger communities, such as Chippenham, had their own priest appointed by a bishop, and the community had probably built and maintained a meeting house there on the site of the present parish church.

To support a church and its priest, the system of tithing was expanded by the bishops of the church to be officially approved by King Edgar in 970. Tithes were the donation of a landholder and his tenants of a tenth of the value of the yearly produce of their land. This was a tax of great value, and a clear demarcation to determine the jurisdiction of each priest's tithing was long overdue. So parishes were created, by deciding which land around a community or estate was to be under the jurisdiction of the local priest, and this land then became a parish unit. The boundaries surrounding each parish defined the land from which the local priest could demand the tithes due. Community by community, over the 10th and 11th centuries, parish boundaries were created, and one of these was the boundary drawn at Cocklebury. It favoured Chippenham, for the parish there was to receive the major share of the tithes from the valuable meadowlands by the Avon.

A ceremony of walking the new parish boundaries to ensure their continuing exactness was created and held each year in almost every parish in England. There were breaks during the walk for refreshments at certain markers, in order to impress their whereabouts on the walkers. This ceremony was sadly neglected at Chippenham by the 17th century, but it can be presumed it was regularly held in medieval times.

The boundary at Cocklebury began in the north-east corner by Peckingell, at a detached section of meadowland there held by Kington St Michael. Proceeding along the course of the Avon, the boundary then crossed the centre of Cocklebury, following the edges of the fields until it reached the track. There it continued on to a point near Chippenham Clift.

Just before the Norman Conquest it can be presumed that the tenants and labourers of Cocklebury were divided in their place of worship. They either crossed the river to attend services in Chippenham church, or walked to Langley to join their lord, Ulwi. The meeting place there was no doubt close by Ulwi's dwelling place, so he could attend services easily. Later, on the site of the meeting place, the foundations of the present Saxon church at Langley Burrell were probably laid.

Because of its close proximity to Chippenham, and its lack of a church or estate house, there was no nucleus for the communities at Cocklebury to cluster around and eventually form a village in the present sense of the word. In later written records, the area was to be known as 'Cocklebury in Chippenham parish' and as 'Cocklebury in Langley Burrell parish'. As the population grew, several settlements formed there, but none, as far as can be ascertained, were to be known by any other name than that of Cocklebury.

Communications within such settlements as Cocklebury would be by footpath from dwelling to dwelling. Certain other paths were used by workers to reach common grazing and cultivation areas. Public footpaths or right of way across these areas and other land was apparently an unknown concept, and for an outsider to trespass probably a crime.

Near to Cocklebury, Chippenham served as a cross-roads of the area. The way from London to the West passed through Chippenham to take advantage of its river crossing, and two routes running up and down the Vale merged there. The present category A roads, except for the road to Bath, follow the same routes as those in Saxon times. The paths from settlements and hamlets around Chippenham that led into these ways were primitive narrow tracks, those over the clays being almost impassable in winter. They have survived today as the narrow, twisting lanes of the countryside.

On the eve of the Norman Conquest, there is no doubt that Chippenham had become a busy place and was the hub of the mid-Vale area. Two centuries of peace and subsequent prosperity had followed King Alfred's successful campaign against the Danes which had culminated in his victory at Edington, and the Danes' later retreat from Chippenham in 878. Besides being the head of a Wiltshire Hundred, a division of local government, Chippenham was the centre of a thriving agricultural area and an important marketing community. Barley, oats, cattle and other farm stock were no doubt sold there, in adition to cheese and butter. The market is also likely to have served as a collection point for fleeces eventually to be shipped to the Continent. Although it is on record that woollen cloths, besides fleeces, were being traded from England to northern European countries in Saxon times, there are no documents to indicate that the West Country woollen industry had yet begun.

At this point it is interesting to consider the likely origins of the name of Chippenham. In King Alfred's will of 873, the spelling indicates the name was *Cippanhamme*. *Hamme* is an Old English suffix used to mean meadow or land enclosed by a river, true of the site of the town to this day. *Ceap* was the Anglo-Saxon word for merchandise, hence the name as a whole seems to indicate a trading centre in the bend of the Avon, a valid description for the Saxon community there.

One of the most important things linking Cocklebury with Chippenham and Langley was the common field system established there in Saxon times. Recent studies on field patterns in parts of Wessex have revealed that the Saxons, instead of continuing their custom of farming small rectangular fields as they did in their Germanic homelands, adopted the British system of strip and open fields inherited from the Romans. At Cocklebury, as in other parts of the Vale, both types of fields evolved, and from records originating in the 12th century, it can be presumed that the common field system is likely to have been well established at Cocklebury by the end of Saxon rule.

These open fields, made up of meadow land by the river and strips of arable land elsewhere, covered much of the total acreage of Cocklebury. The fields were attached either to Chippenham or to Langley, depending in which parish they lay. Along the parish boundary towards the river lay enclosed rectangular fields cultivated by the smallholders of the area. This landscape at Cocklebury was to remain practically unchanged until the reign of Henry VIII.

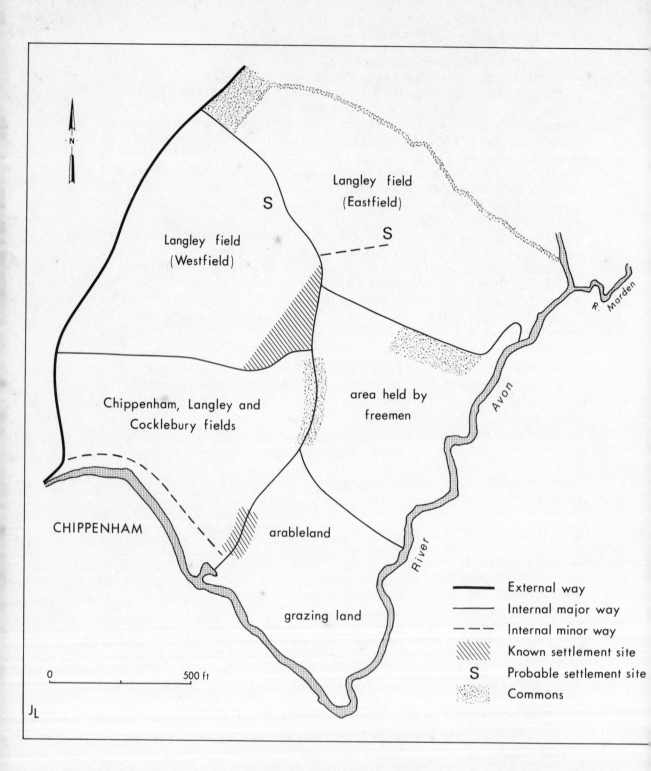

Medieval Fields around Cocklebury

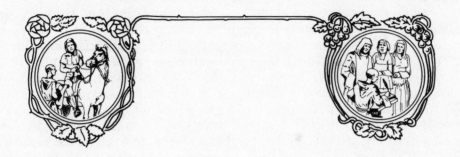

Chapter Three

1066 to the Black Death

So far as can be ascertained, the coming of the Normans to Wiltshire was a far more peaceable conquest than that of the Saxons 500 years before. The first major change in the lives of the people was the replacement of their estate lord. At Cocklebury, the life of the labourer was to be more severely governed by the rules of a new feudal society brought over by the Normans, but the small holders retained their holdings and were free men by the 12th century, if not before.

One of King William's first actions towards governing his new kingdom was to replace most of the Saxon estate-holders by men of his own country. There is a correlation in some counties of England between the amount of opposition offered to the Normans and the number of Saxons allowed to retain a part of their estate. The less the opposition, the greater the number of Saxon landholders remaining after the Conquest. If this correlation is valid, then the occupation of Wiltshire and its later division by the Normans after 1066 was a peaceful affair.

The replacement of the Saxon landlords was a comparatively simple political move designed to provide the new aristocracy with an immediate stake in their new country. It placed them, as representatives of the Crown, in close contact with the Saxon society they were to rule. Their feudal system not only laid down explicitly the obligations of a tenant to a landlord, and his obligations to the king, but it also defined the responsibilities of a landholder to his tenants and workers on his new manor, as the Saxon estates were now to be called.

After a decade or so, these changes in government brought into focus the necessity for a survey of all the landholdings in the kingdom. The chief aim of the survey was to provide information on which to create a new tax structure, greatly needed to regularly provision the King's perpetually empty Exchequer. The result of this survey was in time to be called the Domesday (i.e. Day of Judgement) Survey or Domesday Book.[1]

To make the survey, appointed commissioners and their clerks began travelling in specified circuits through the countryside to obtain information from landlords or their agents, regarding their holdings. In addition, chosen representatives from each county Hundred gave evidence on oath to supplement the details obtained from the circuits. The testimony obtained was sent to Exchequer clerks at Winchester, transcribed, grouped into counties and their Hundreds and assembled into book form. Despite the poor roads and difficult communications of the times, the survey was completed within a year, and taxes based upon it were being received within a few months after its final assembly. There were 569 entries for Wiltshire, mostly of manorial holdings. The list of landholders began with the King, was followed by ecclesiastics, nobles and commoners, and ended with certain servants of the King's household. Each holding was documented and described with its value and the assessed tax or due to be paid by it.

Cocklebury is not listed in the Domesday Book, for it was not a separate estate at the time. By geographical location, however, it was included in the Survey within the manors of Chippenham and Langley. The boundaries of both these manors, but more certainly of Langley manor, are likely to have been much the same as their parish boundaries, hence the inclusion of Cocklebury within both of them. (For the Chippenham and Langley Domesday Book entries, see Appendix A.) According to the Domesday Book, Chippenham manor was retained by the King, probably because of its convenient proximity to the hunting grounds of the royal forest which formed much of the manor's boundary. As a consequence, the manor was taxed by the obligation to provision the monarch and his court for 24 hours when visiting Chippenham. How often the people of Chippenham (and of course, these included the people of Cocklebury south of the parish boundary there) fulfilled their obligation cannot be known, but as they were always threatened by bad harvests and the spectre of famine, they probably hoped that it would not be too frequently.

Langley became one of the estates received by Edward, Earl of Salisbury and Sheriff of Wiltshire, as one of his rewards for his support to the Crown. In turn, the Earl rented Langley to Borel (here is the origin of Langley Burrell), who replaced Ulwi, the Saxon lord. It is interesting to note that Ulwi was not completely dispossessed, for he was allowed to retain one hide of good land. In both entries there is a wealth of detail concerning the various strata of labourers. It can be presumed such strata existed at Cocklebury, husbanding its land with oxen and plough, making hay and grazing cattle in its meadowland.

Twelve mills are recorded at Chippenham. They were located along the Avon, or close by on a tributary. Among them were at least two known to be at Cocklebury, one later on record as belonging to the leading family of free men there, the de Cockleburys, the other a corn mill by the river crossing at Chippenham, a site where corn was ground until the present century. Such a large number of mills for the small town Chippenham appears to have been at the time is certainly an indication of its prosperity. Another mill, recorded in the Domesday entry for Kington St Michael, was located on the river at Peckingell, just north of Cocklebury, where the parish of Kington St Michael held a detached portion of meadowland.

The Domesday Survey states that Chippenham parish church had held a considerable amount of land since Saxon times. Later church records suggest that a part of this land was likely to have been portions of meadowland and common field at Cocklebury, a tradition of land holding to survive there until the 18th century.

Two individual landholders are cited in the entry for Chippenham; Rainald Canut held one hide, and Roger of Berkley held a portion of the demesne farm. The former does not appear again, but the Berkeleys of Gloucestershire do. They later paid feudal dues on Langley manor, and intermarriage with the de Cobhams, Langley's manor lords in the 14th century, sustained their interest there for 500 years.

In the 12th century the manors of Chippenham and Langley consolidated into feudal units, with their hierarchy of labourers, artisans, freemen, bailiffs, and manor lords; in addition, within the town of Chippenham were merchants and their employees. Such a social order seemed set to endure for ever. Each man had his duties and obligations to his manor, each man had his rights. All were spelt out by ancient custom and upheld by the manorial court.

A record of such customs from Chippenham manor has survived, incorporated into a 13th-century rent roll, though the customs are undoubtedly of a much earlier date.[2] It is apparent that the services required by the manor lord were to take priority over the husbanding of the labourers' own holdings. The principal rent payers, who held a virgate of land or more, had to plough the lord's land with their own oxen. In addition, if they possessed horses as well, they also had to harrow the land after ploughing. For that duty, their pay was one meal a day. At planting time, women were employed, their reward being 'all they could drink' (cider and perry?). All labourers on the manor had to hoe the resulting plants until they were cleared of weeds, the pay being two pence.

Later on in the season, haymaking–the cutting, the tossing and the carrying of it to the barn or rick–was worth 6d and a share of the hay. At harvest time, each man was to reap half an acre a day, worth 13 sheaves of the corn. Reaping was forbidden on Saturdays, perhaps because the hard labour it entailed demanded an extra day of rest. The sheaves were to be taken to the barn in the lord's cart, a task paying a sheaf a day. The stubble after harvesting was to be cut at the rate of half an acre a day for no pay, but probably the cut stubble was a perquisite of the labourers, as were the gleaning rights after the corn was cut.

In the following farming year at the time of sowing, each man had to thrash a bushel of corn a day, his earnings to be only a farthing. (This rate of pay sounds sheer exploitation, for thrashing with a flail was considered the hardest agricultural work of all, even more tiring than scything grass.) Other duties included the dipping and shearing of the lord's sheep, the men so employed to receive one cream cheese and a portion of the sheared wool. When timber was to be cut from the forest, the labourers were allowed two meals a day, and a load of timber. A herdsman was given a halfpenny a beast, for watching the cattle and preventing them from straying from their grazing area. The reward for tending the lord's sheep or pigs was one lamb or piglet, the second best of the year. In addition, for the man who tended the pigs, there was the privilege of receiving the by-products of the annual pig killing, leaving the bacon and the lard for the lord. As a guideline to the value of the pay for all these manorial duties, the average rent for a dwelling paid to Chippenham manor was, according to this rent roll, 8d a quarter, or 32d a year.

During the 12th century a change in land holding occurred at Cocklebury, a change to alter the course of its history thereafter. In 1150, the Crown presented land at Cocklebury in Chippenham parish to Farleigh Priory, a newly-established religious house five miles from Bath. Gifts such as this were not a prerogative of the Crown only, and were, of course, no new phenomenon to the area. The great pre-Conquest Abbeys of Malmesbury and Glastonbury retained extensive holdings near Chippenham, and after the Conquest, French religious houses were encouraged by the King to expand, and to set up daughter houses in England. This they did, with the result that by the end of the 13th century, nearly half of the countryside was in the hands of ecclesiastical organisations. Great rivalry occurred among the various religious orders for land, and at Cocklebury, three monasteries were involved: Farleigh Priory of the Cluniac order; Bradenstoke Priory, founded by Augustinian canons; and Stanley Abbey, a Cistercian house.

Farleigh Priory ultimately held the largest amount of land at Cocklebury. It was founded in 1120, and soon after its patron family, the de Bohuns, who had followed the Conqueror to England, bestowed upon it the manor and village of Farleigh. In the years following, the same family donated many other gifts of land and property to the Priory, but it was the Empress Matilda who gave it 'Monkton, juxta Chippenham, Wilts'. The name Monkton, apparently used here for the first time, was seldom seen again until the manor of Monkton was created there in 1536.

As was the custom, the Priory made larger gifts of land into farms, each to be run as a unit employing local labourers already on the land, with a bailiff to supervise. Besides the home farm at Farleigh, the Priory ran nine other farms in north Wiltshire. They included one at Thornehill, on the edge of Langley Burrell, and others at Allington, and at Monkton near

Broughton Gifford, Melksham. And, of course, there was Cocklebury, which was called Chippenham manor, though it was not the Chippenham manor *per se*. That was held by a noble in 1299, the Earl of Cornwall. But the farm was undoubtedly run as a manorial unit, adhering to such working customs as previously described in this chapter.

The farm's acreage at Cocklebury consisted of land around the site of Monkton House today, incorporating portions of both common field and meadowland. To the north, it was probably bounded by a hedge that extended from the Avon by Matford field to a point near Chippenham Clift. A portion of this hedge still exists, and recent species count indicated it was certainly in existence by 1200.

A description of the farm has survived, for it was valued with the Priory's other units in 1294. One of the certifiers of its value was a Humphrey Payne of Cocklebury, a family name which will be heard of again. The farm consisted of 124 acres of arable land and 14 acres of meadow. The acreage of arable land probably included land held by the monastery across the river from Chippenham. The labour force was recorded as eight free tenants, seven villeins and cottagers. The free tenants paid their rent in money only, the others in money and services. The farm used three teams of oxen, one mule and two horses for carting. There were 33 cows and young cattle and 63 pigs. Despite a rainy summer, a surplus of wheat, barley, oats, beans and hay had been produced that year. A statistical analysis of the 1294 crop yields of the nine Priory farms, taking into consideration such variables as acreages, labour employed and animals used indicates that yields at Cocklebury were considerably higher than any of the other units, a tribute to Cocklebury's fertile lands and the efficiency of the Priory's bailiff.

A house for that bailiff, with a garden and pigeonry, had been included in the valuation. In the records of the later Monkton manor, there is a reference to 'the site of an ancient farmhouse' just east of the present Monkton House. Also located in the same area is a piece of meadowland, known in the 19th century as Pigeon House field. In all likelihood, the bailiff's house was on the site of this ancient farmhouse, and his pigeonry in the area of the field. Certainly this would have been a suitable location, for it lay in the centre of the Priory's land at Cocklebury, and only a short journey from its holdings at Chippenham.

Although its holdings at Cocklebury did not in any way rival the size of those of Farleigh Priory, Bradenstoke Priory also acquired land there in the 12th and 13th centuries. The Priory was situated on the edge of the Vale, six miles north of Cocklebury, and its major holdings were close by; but it particularly valued meadowland and rich pastures, so it was willing to acquire such land in small parcels, often quite distant from Bradenstoke. In this respect it competed with Malmesbury Abbey as its holdings were interwoven amongst holdings of the much earlier-established religious houses.

In 1232, Nicholas de Cokelburg gave the Priory two acres of land in Eastwell, a field near Cocklebury, and allowed the Abbot to purchase three more acres nearby. This acreage may have been rented out, or perhaps a certain number of animals, the property of the Priory, grazed there under the eye of a local shepherd or herdsman. The Priory was also granted pasture in the royal enclosure of Chippenham forest 'for 2 bulls, 40 cows and their year-old calves', plus meadowland at Barrows farm, Langley Burrell, just opposite Cocklebury land.

Stanley Abbey, the third religious house with holdings at Cocklebury in medieval times, was founded just a little too late to acquire very much land there. The Abbey, a daughter house of Quarr Abbey on the Isle of Wight, was first established in 1153 at Loxwell by 'a singular and romantic spring on the summit of a hill in Pewsham forest'. Three years later the community moved to Stanley, within a mile of the River Avon at Cocklebury. Various explanations have been offered for this move, but the light soils and level land by the banks of the Marden and Avon were probably responsible. The Cistercians were known for the intensively cultivated and orderly farm granges attached to their monasteries, and the area at Stanley was superior for this purpose to the sloping lands of Loxwell. Once at Stanley, the order received many gifts of land, buildings, and rents from royal and private benefactors.

By comparison with other Cistercian houses, especially those in Yorkshire, Stanley had few granges, and relied heavily on its 450-acre home farm to produce its food and other agricultural products. It is likely that the Abbey also produced woollen cloth, for its mill in 1189 was documented as a fulling mill, one of the earliest known in England. There is no doubt that the Abbey would have found land at Cocklebury an easily-accessible addition to their home farm. But it is not until 1185, 30 years after its founding, that any records of the Abbey's holdings at Cocklebury are found; a small amount of meadowland and a mill rent donated by the de Cocklebury family. Later, the same family gave the Abbey more pasture at Eastmead, a common grazing area across the river. The Abbey's Cartulary, dated 1236, also records 'Thomas de la Mare de quodam prato extra Chippeham super ripam fluminis Avene. Et vocatur Dounham'. [Thomas de la Mare, a certain extent of meadowland away from Chippenham on the edge of the Avon. And also named Downham.] This land was also at Cocklebury.

In the 13th century the religious houses transferred land at Cocklebury among themselves, gathering small parcels together for easier management, by exchanging one or two acres for others more conveniently located. In 1245, Bradenstoke Priory gave Stanley three acres of arable land while relinquishing two acres and 'rights in Alfredmore wood by the Abbey gate'. By such means, at the end of the century Cocklebury was consolidated between the three religious houses, the two manors of Chippenham and Langley Burrell, and the freeholders. There was little hope for any ambitious labourer of acquiring a smallholding for himself, in order to gain a measure of independence.

The freeholders, however, had become the owners of their land. The most prominent of them, the de Cocklebury family, were first recorded in 1181 as paying their taxes to the Sheriff of Wiltshire. A few years later, Simon, then patriarch of the family, with his son Peter, gave to Stanley Abbey the rents from land and a mill at Cocklebury. The yearly rent of the mill was 10s and 'a stick of eels' (but the length of the stick was not specified!) Fifty years later Nicholas, grandson of Simon, was still donating these rents to the Abbey, though disputing with the Abbot the ownership of the mill.

In 1241, five years after his disagreement with the Abbot, Nicholas appeared before a court again in a land dispute, one continuing for eight years. Nicholas defended (against a John Pritchard and his wife, Ela, also residents of Cocklebury), a claim for two messuages and one virgate of land. John thought that a 'fine' (an agreement) brought before a special court at Wilton near Salisbury had permitted him to farm fields at Manniscroft, which had been common land when the fine was enacted. The field name of Mancroft often denoted common, or land accessible to all, lying on a parish boundary, which is where the field named Manniscroft lay at Cocklebury. But Nicholas had stopped John by force of arms from grazing his beasts there. John, in defence, complained that Nicholas had houses, buildings and a fish pond in adjoining pastures, inferring Nicholas also farmed there, and that he, John, had also rented a farm at Cocklebury to William le Oyselr for eight years at 3s a year. Ralph, Nicholas's son, had on his father's orders, ejected William and would not allow John onto the land again, or reimburse him for his lost rents.

Nicholas claimed damages of 100s, plus 4s 6d lost rents. The case was settled by agreement, after the jury had supported Nicholas's claim that Manniscroft was not common land anymore. Ralph said he would pay John 3s a year rent and arrears, and Nicholas put forth one mark (5s 9d) for court fees. What William le Oyselr felt about his lost farm is unlikely to be discovered. The family stayed at Cocklebury though, for in 1310, a deed records a grant by Richard att Botte to William Oly and his wife Agnes, for 'land in Cockelborghe part lying in Langley Burrell', not too far from the originally-disputed farms.[2]

The appearance of these small farmers (for the acreages involved could hardly be more than 10) in this dispute indicate they were freeholders, not villeins, having their land for life, with conveyance rights to their heirs. The desciption of the case gives an impression of their prosperity, independence and assurance. All were prepared to take a dispute to a court 25 miles away, and to continue it for several years.

Court proceedings such as this are recorded as 'Feet of Fines'. They dealt with transactions in land. The fine described the final agreement, written in triplicate, on a single parchment. The parchment was then indented, i.e. cut in a wavy line, to avoid fraud and to divide each copy of the agreement. The copy at the bottom of the parchment, written at a right angle to the other two copies on the body of the parchment, was retained by the court and known as the foot. The parties to the agreement (in the above case Nicholas de Cocklebury and the Pritchards), each took a copy above the foot. Hence the documents retained by the court came to be known as Feet of Fines. By contrast, the document giving title to the land, known as a Deed Poll, was so called as no duplicate was needed and hence its edges were trimmed straight, i.e. polled. Feet of Fines are an excellent source material for local historians, for besides ownership, they often recorded topgraphical information and field and family names. Later on, such disputes were frequently used to record officially a person's claim to particular lands (this occurred twice in two decades after a family named Goldney had first bought land at Cocklebury in the 16th century), and genuine disputes become fewer in Feet of Fines records.

Another court used for land disputes was the Eyre for Common Pleas. It was a royal court held by the King's justices in different counties at intervals of several years, and was the chief institution for the administration of justice in the 12th and 13th centuries. In 1249, the Wiltshire Eyre was part of a countrywide visitation conducted by groups of judges who travelled on circuits. At this court, before the Crown Pleas division, William, son of Matthew Lanngel, established claim to one virgate in Langley, his claim being backed by his neighbours, Roger le Mariscal of Chipha, and John le Fraunkeleir of Cokeberge.

Another family name, Payne, crops up frequently in conjunction with both Cocklebury and Chippenham. Payne's close or leaze lay just north-east of Cocklebury farmhouse. Richard le Eveshe, in 1232, gave a 6d rent to Bradenstoke Priory for a messuage which Payn de Chipeham held. As Payne's leaze lay on the Chippenham side of the parish boundary, this is likely to be the same land. Humphrey de Payne, who had appeared as a certifier to the value of Farleigh Priory's farm at Cocklebury in 1294, frequently upheld statements at Inquisitions Post Mortem held at Chippenham. (I.P.M.s were held in front of a body of reputable local men to ensure the correct inheritance of the King's land after its holder had died. The proceedings were recorded and later filed in London. They served in many instances in lieu of a birth certificate, a type of record not in existence at the time.)

In the next century the Paynes were to expand their interests into Chippenham, where they paid 2s 2d for the rent of a house, which they probably sublet. They also hired a stall in the Market Place. There is no clue as to what they sold there, but it could have been woollen cloth. Their holdings at Cocklebury remained in the family, for in 1604 Roger Payne of Cockleborowe appears on a Chippenham tax list, and in 1583 the same Roger, or his father, had been fined 12d for trespassing in Manningcroft. Obviously the area was still a bone of contention, although more than three centuries had elapsed since the court case concerning the field had taken place between Nicholas de Cocklebury and the Pritchards.

A case concerning Cocklebury appears in Feet of Fines records for 1341. This case is obviously for determining ownership of land, as the areas are defined in what was, for that time, great detail, and no references are made to misdemeanours or disagreements. Walter de Haywoode is the plaintiff, and the defendants are Nicholas de Haywoode and his wife Joan. The basic claim is for eight houses, a carucate of land, 10 acres of meadowland (of which three were in Cocklebury) and 20s of rents, the whole in Langgelegh, Chippenham and Cokelberwe. This description fits land in the north of Cocklebury. The Haywood family survived the ravages of the Black Death, and prospered, but they only appear in Chippenham records thereafter. A Walter Haywood rented land there in 1353 and 1371, and a Robert Hayward is collector of rents for Chippenham manor in 1427, a position he held for several years. And along with Walter Haywood in the 1371 rent roll appears a new name–Nicholas Gale. Here is the first known mention of a family encountered in all records of Cocklebury until the 19th century, and in Chippenham to the present day.

One other name deserves mention, for it survives at Cocklebury today. Between 1370 and 1386 a John Rawlyn lived at Cocklebury, presumably in the vicinity of the site of the present farmhouse there that now bears his name. John and any other member of his family do not appear again in records so far examined, but the name, retained at Cocklebury as a place name, begins to appear after the 16th century.

In the mid-1300s, on the eve of the Black Death, Chippenham parish church had accumulated many gifts of land, donated by citizens. Several of these gifts lay in Cocklebury, such as the one acre of land lying in Odecroft, a close of William Payne, together with an acre of Cocklebury in Gandersdyke near the grange of William le Marceshel, and a close lying 'near the King's highway', the road to Wootten Bassett. Other gifts followed in the 15th century, usually small acreages in the common fields at Cocklebury, of Chippenham and Langley Burrell. Because of lack of maps until the 18th century, names such as Mor furlong, Nethercliffe, Sanders-ditch, and Westbrook identified these sections and they remained in use until enclosure took place much later. Often with the name of the section was a description of its location which now provides a clue to the position of the common fields at the time. 'The third part of one ham of meadow in Langley field near Felditch one head thereof extending upon the bank of the Avon' shows that Langley East field did stretch to the Avon and included grazing lands there. Other information, such as place name origins can be obtained: 'one acre of arable land in Cockelburg, lying under a certain place called the Clyve', is evidence of the origin of the naming of Chippenham Clift, for it is derived from the French word 'cleeve', meaning fissure, and not from cliff, as could be presumed from the terrain.

Chapter Four

To the Threshold of Change

The appearance of the Black Death in Europe in 1348, taken in conjunction with the six subsequent outbreaks over the next 50 years, was the most lethal disaster in the history of mankind up to the First World War. In England the Black Death killed one person in three, and its impact reached everywhere, even to such small communities as Cocklebury. No words can describe the feelings of fear and terror an outbreak of the disease evoked. As it spread across the countryside, a person had to face the possibility of an agonising death, conveyed by unexplained forces, to strike at an untold time. After it had passed, the survivors had to withstand the anguish of loss of family and work companions, a breakdown of day-to-day life, and the threat of famine if the crops were not planted. For the smallholders, the loss of family labour and harvests could mean in time the surrender of their land, for they seldom had the financial capital to carry them through so many disastrous years. For the upper classes, the question of inheritance and of finding the ways and the means to work their land became of prime importance; and like the common man's, the collapse of their society and the uncertain future made life hard to endure.

But out of the disaster came one consequence which today would be considered a benefit. The Black Death precipitated England onto the rocky path leading to democracy. The feudal system was torn apart, and the hold of the aristocracy on the common worker was weakened. After 1350, a man found it much easier to leave his home manor, to move to a town and find a living there. Or he could go to another manor or village, and better himself by becoming an artisan or craftsman. If he remained on his home manor, he could, due to the shortage of labour, bid for a higher wage, the wage to be paid in money only. He could resist demands on his services in lieu of rent if he held land which he tilled for himself. All these events took place at

Cocklebury as elsewhere. Both manor lords and their families were afflicted by the Black Death in the first or a subsequent outbreak, some of the smallholders lost their land, and feudalism was greatly weakened.

The plague, or pestilence as it was called at the time, first appeared in England at Dorset in the summer of 1348. It was brought from the Continent by shipboard rats infected with fleas, which in turn carried the disease bacillus–*Yersinia pestis*–to human beings. Slowly it spread across southern England to the west, reaching Bristol at the beginning of 1349. Here 'it raged to such a degree that the living were scarce able to bury their dead, and . . . the grass grew several inches high in the High Street and Broad Street'. From Bristol the plague continued to the city of Gloucester, probably again carried on small ships or boats sailing between the two cities. Citizens of Gloucester attempted to close their city gates to refugees from Bristol, a vain effort. Inexorably, the plague continued across the countryside to North Wiltshire. It lingered there from February to September, the most important months of the farming year, meanwhile spreading further east towards London and south deeper into Wiltshire. There was to be no escape for the people of the county.

Around Cocklebury many manors suffered. Hugh le Despenser died at Sherston near Malmesbury on 8 February 1349, and his nephew Edward, aged 12, inherited the manor. Six days later Eleanor Gacelyn of Chippenham died, leaving her son Edmund to inherit. John Oliver of Cocklebury was one who later swore that Edmund was the legal heir to the manor. Such deaths occurred all over the county in 1349, 1361 and again in 1369. Many manors were not inherited by the customary eldest son–often an infant son, a daughter, or even a distant relative received a manor, an indication that many or all members of the family living at a manor had died.

As a result of the plague, manors also lost their tenants. At Roger Normand's manor near Wootton Bassett (to be inherited by a grandson aged five), all the tenants died except for three freeholders. At other manors, there were no rents paid 'because all the tenants of the manor are in Berkshire'. And 'tenements are worth nothing because they are unoccupied and cannot be sold for want of buyers'. At Calstone near Calne, the watermill of the manor was 'broken down and worthless', and one third of the tenants and their families had died. Langley Burrell's lord, Sir Reginald de Cobham, survived the plague of 1349, only to succumb in 1361, at the time of its second round in Wiltshire.

Monastic houses were particularly afflicted, because of their duty to the sick and the danger of a rapidly-spreading infection if one of their members came down with the disease. Thirteen out of 14 brothers of Ivy Church Priory in southern Wiltshire died, and the remaining member requested the Bishop of Salisbury that he be made Prior. His request was granted. If Farleigh Priory suffered such a loss, the affairs of their farm at Cocklebury would have been sadly neglected, even more so if the bailiff there was also stricken.

It is obvious that the plague disrupted the lives of those at Cocklebury. It would be impossible to find labour to plant the corn and vetches, to cut and carry the hay. And the following years when labour might have been obtainable, there were two disastrously wet summers, creating famine conditions each winter. The next 25 years saw a period of unsettled weather and many poor harvests, further hindering the return to any semblance of everyday living. But although life was never to be the same again, recovery at Cocklebury did take place. There is little doubt that as soon as possible the fields at Cocklebury were tilled again, and the cattle and other animals replaced. (Reputedly, they too died of the plague and many must also have died of neglect.) Chippenham itself still flourished, as one of the centres of the West County woollen industry. Its prosperity probably helped to attract labourers from devastated manors to the town, and if they did not find employment in the woollen trades, they no doubt could work in the nearby fields, including those at Cocklebury.

A recent claim that Cocklebury became a deserted medieval village, ceasing to exist after the Black Death, has little justification. Life continued there. A tax roll of 1377 for instance, records ten persons or households liable for payment. (Whether they could pay their taxes is another matter.) This is the same number of households recorded there in the years just before the Black Death, but it is not known whether the households were the same. However, the names of such families as de Cocklebury, le Mareschel, Champion, Rawlyn and Pritchard are seen no more in local records after the plague years.

After these years there is little mention of Cocklebury in any secular records until the 16th century. The reason for this, however, is that Farleigh Priory began to add to its land holdings there, in both parishes of Chippenham and Langley Burrell. It seems too, that in time the Priory also obtained nearly all of the land there that was once farmed by the smallholders. In 1392 the Priory accepted gifts of land at Cocklebury from a John Gore. A few years later a Simon Porter donated lands at Cocklebury in Langley Burrell. Simon may have lost his wife from the plague, for in return for these lands the Priory had to accept Simon and his son into their community at Farleigh, and to give to his heirs 'a belt and a knife at Michaelmas'.

In the Wiltshire Record Office is a parchment of 1417 recording in gold ink and beautiful script the 'rents received by the Priory of Farleigh at Chippenham Cokeburgh and Barrow'. This is the earliest evidence of Farleigh renting out Cocklebury land, a custom that was to continue until the dissolution of the Priory. But it probably began after 1349, and the Priory's farm was broken up and leased out in sections at about the same time.

In later years the more prosperous citizens of Chippenham began to combine their trade of merchant or clothier with farming. They rented land in the town's common fields and pastures, and such land included that at Cocklebury belonging to the Priory. Its final rent roll, compiled in 1536, shows that sections of arable fields, pasture, 'mede' and Cocklebury Common were being held by various local individuals, some leases running as long as 70 years.

The Priory did not make good use of its rents, for it had a history of financial disaster all through the 15th century. In 1462 it had not paid dues to the lord of Chippenham manor for several years, and owed 'by reason of their insufficiency' nearly twenty five shillings. Ten years later the Priory was described as 'destitute of all virtue and good rule', a portrayal which at the time applied to many religious houses throughout England.

So farming continued at Cocklebury in the 15th century, apparently peacefully and unhurried. The following century was to see the beginning of radical changes in the fabric of life in England, changes that were to lead the people of Cocklebury into modern times.

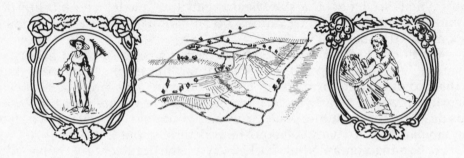

Chapter Five

The Beginning of Modern Farming at Cocklebury

The 16th century was a turning point in the story of Cocklebury. Most of the common field area was enclosed and small farms were created, their new fields clustered around a central farmhouse. Such a drastic alteration in the landscape at Cocklebury was to be made possible by a change in the ownership of land there, from ecclesiastical to secular, and by the increasing fortunes of three families who were to make their homes at Cocklebury through the century.

The previous century had seen the gradual economic demise of the religious establishments of England. It was this demise, combined with other religious, social and economic reasons, that by 1536 brought the Reformation into being; it is a misconception that Henry VIII's need to divorce Catherine of Aragon in order to marry Ann Boleyn was the primary cause. For over a century, the feeling had existed among both nobles and commoners that religious houses were no longer fulfilling their spiritual duties. Nearly half the lands of England were held by the Church, and the wasteful management of them was quite blatant, an aggravation to those not so well off or so rich in land, and to those without any land at all, who coveted them. Pressure, both political and economic, was being put on the Crown by men who had acquired wealth by trade and wanted a country estate. There were courtiers and servants around the King who realised the economic gain to the country and to themselves if the ecclesiastical lands were to be distributed among them. Henry VIII, always a greedy man, wanted more power and revenue. If the monasteries were dissolved, the political power of the Catholic Church would be transferred to him; the clamour for religious reform would be satisfied; and the spiritual influence of the Catholic Church would, he thought, be broken once and for all. The Church's buildings and possessions could be sold, and the lands (of which Cocklebury was a typical example) besides enriching the king and his subjects by the transferrence of their ownership, could be taxed to provide a constant revenue. It all seemed to point to a simple and timely solution. So the Dissolution of the Monasteries began, and was carried out in the course of a few years.

Plans were made by the Crown to investigate the affairs of the religious establishments, and a financial appraisal known as the *Valor Ecclesiasticus* appeared in early 1536. Soon after the actual confiscation of the houses began although some, despite the haste with which the government was acting, were in a greater hurry to surrender. Stanley Abbey did so just after the appearance of *Valor Ecclesiasticus*, but Farleigh Priory hung on. It was suppressed in time for its lands to be granted to Edward Seymour in June 1536, three weeks after the marriage of his sister Jane to King Henry. After this marriage, Edward Seymour became one of the most powerful men in the kingdom. He bore many titles in his lifetime, Viscount Beauchamp, Earl of Hertford, Duke of Somerset, and finally, Lord Protector of England. He and his descendants play an important role in the story of Cocklebury, for their financial and political misfortunes led eventually to the return of Cocklebury, after 150 years, to closer management under local ownership.

Seymour had spent his childhood in Wiltshire, at Wolf Hall, near Marlborough. A close friend and hard-working servant of Henry VIII, in reward for his services Seymour had received a considerable amount of ecclesiastical land appropriated by the Crown for various reasons several years before the Dissolution. His sister's marriage increased his favour with the King, and the June 1536 grant was one of the many awarded to him. In total, these grants could have made him one of the richest men in England, but as fast as he obtained land, he sold or mortgaged it, in order to pay off endless debts that never seemed to cease accumulating.

Seymour acquired Cocklebury when all the lands of Farleigh Priory were granted to him. Detailed planning by his steward, Berwick, had preceded this grant, so that small parcels of land belonging to other religious houses adjoining Farleigh lands had also been collected and added to the grant. In the neighbourhood of Cocklebury, this meant the lands of Stanley across the Avon and south of the Abbey and several messuages and gardens in Chippenham. Bradenstoke land at Cocklebury was not included in the grant, for the Prior, a stubborn and determined man, held out against the King's Commissioners until he was forced to surrender in 1539. Only then did Seymour obtain these lands.

An interesting study could be made by recording the disposition of all the monastical lands in Wiltshire, and then enumerating the resulting estates a hundred years later. The creation of Monkton manor at Cocklebury and the small working estate that finally emerged is an example. Another estate created was that of Easton manor near Marlborough. It was formerly part of the lands of Easton Priory, also granted to Seymour in 1536. His steward, John Berwick, had aided 'the speedy dissolution of the houses of Farleigh' and otherwise hastened the process of assembling monastic lands for Seymour's grants. Four years later, Berwick was to be described as 'John Barwick of Eston, Wilts, esquire'. So the manor was sold or given by Seymour to Berwick, with the result that he apparently became one of the 'landed gentry'.

Out of the Farleigh lands Seymour acquired at Cocklebury, Chippenham, Langley and Stanley, the manor of Monkton was created, a small estate among many others that he at one time possessed in Wiltshire. That Seymour ever visited the manor was doubtful, for it was Berwick who rode between his estates, supervising their bailiffs, arranging farm supplies, preparing accounts, and even mustering men for service in the militia. An early rent roll gives details of the leases held on the land incorporated into Monkton manor. Most of the acreage of the original Priory farm was held by a Richard Apharry. In 1539 he was appointed by the Seymour estate to be rent collector for Broughton Gifford, and bailiff in charge of lands that were once of the original nine Priory farms. A busy man, Apharry still retained his tenancy at Cocklebury until 1545, when he headed a list of taxpayers there. The list also included Thomas Scott and Henry Goldney, two family names to be associated with the area until the 18th century.

After Jane Seymour's son came to the throne in 1547 as Edward VI, Seymour, his uncle, became Lord Protector of England. He also became, in fact, if not in title, the first Protestant ruler of England. However, his desire for extreme religious reform, and his lack of political astuteness brought about his downfall. His enemies, all powerful families of the kingdom, eager to assume his authority, plotted his demise. Eventually he was arrested and tried, taken to the Tower of London and beheaded in 1551. His lands were forfeited and he left his 13-year-old heir, Edward, Earl of Hertford, deeply in debt.

During the minority of the Earl of Hertford, Monkton manor was held by a Robert Dyrdo, but by 1559, Gabriel Pleydell was renting the manor. Although a member of the prosperous Pleydell family of Preshute in Wiltshire and Coleshill in Berkshire, Gabriel was in debt. His son, Olivier, took over the tenancy in name, and both father and son became heavily involved with leading local families selling and mortgaging land around Chippenham. There was evidently a certain amount of mismanagement at Monkton, but the arrival of the Bayliffe family there proved to be a steadying influence. It was probably due to a connection with the Pleydell family that originally brought the Bayliffe family to Monkton by 1567. Said to be from Castle Cary, Somerset, William Bayliffe had attended Middle Temple, one of the Inns of Court, with a John Pleydell. Later, William's son married Agnes, a sister of Olivier Pleydell, so the close connection continued for many years.

The young Edward Seymour's estate manager was Sir John Thynne, and with his many connections in Somerset, it may have been he who decided to grant the tenancy of Monkton manor to William Bayliffe. (Sir John later built Longleat House on the borders of Somerset and Wiltshire, and today the library at Longleat houses many Seymour family documents, including records of Monkton manor.) The young Earl was completely dependent on Sir John's management of his affairs, and frequently certain portions of his inheritance were either mortgaged or sold to meet debts. A portion of Cocklebury was severed from Monkton manor for this reason.

The Thynne family was associated in business with the Long and Horton families. All were involved in the woollen trade, and together they played an important role in the economics and politics of north-west Wiltshire. In 1570, at an inquiry before John Thynne and others, it was sworn that William Horton, deeply in debt, had title to two messuages, three tenements, 70 acres of land, 40 acres of meadow and 100 acres of pasture in Chippenham parish. His debts finally caught up with him, for in 1598, he was forced to lease 80 acres of pasture and 20 acres of meadow to 'William Bayliff esquire of Monkton'. Described as land in Cockleborough, in the parish of Chippenham, there is no question that this land was part of the same property as described at the inquiry, and originally belonged to Farleigh Priory.

The lease itself is a mine of information about Cocklebury. The land was farmed by a Simon Sloper, who during his tenancy had to 'repair, maintain and sustain fence, inclosure, hedge and ditch: to cleanse scour and mend them'. William Bayliffe was required to allow William Horton 'the fattinge, feedinge, goeinge and departing of one horse beaste, mare or guildinge from the third day of May untill the fourteenth day of September'. And Horton and his servant were to be permitted to 'put in or fetch out the horse without contradiction, interruption, molestation, vexation or denial by William Bayliffe'. Was this a condition in the lease to ensure Horton had an extra mount during the summer when he had business with clothiers at Chippenham, who no doubt included the Scotts and Goldneys at Cocklebury? The lease continued with conditions for the payment of taxes and tithes, and finished by exhorting William Bayliffe 'to peaceably and quietly have, hold, occupy, possess and enjoy the premises and every part and parcel of the land leased'.

As a result of this 1598 lease, it is possible that the present Cocklebury farmhouse was built. Its form is typical of small farmhouses then being constructed in the southern end of the Cotswold limestone belt, and many similar houses can be found in the same area. It was a simple house (for Simon Sloper?), no more than a large kitchen on the ground floor, with a hearth at one end of the house and an adjoining small buttery at the other. Above, reached by a ladder, was one big sleeping room for the tenant and his family, its Tudor stone fireplace still intact today. In the attic, the space was undoubtedly used to store cheeses, with part of it sectioned off to provide a garret for the farmhouse servants. The layout of the house suggests that on a modest farm–such as this land was at the time–it was not customary for the farm help to live in the same house as the family. They dwelt nearby in those messuages and tenements mentioned at William Horton's inquiry in 1570, or journeyed from Chippenham or Langley Burrell to their work.

Not long after it seems William Bayliffe was able to purchase this land at Cocklebury. In doing so, he laid the foundations for an estate there of his own. He knew the Bayliffe family were going to stay at Monkton, because in 1596, the Seymour family had rented the manor to them for 100 years or three lives, i.e. three generations. The lease included a house, 'edifices', barns, stables and gardens, plus all arable lands, meadows and pastures. William Bayliffe was obligated to maintain these buildings and their grounds. The liberty of fishing in the Avon was extended, as was fowling on the manor lands, but no claim could be made by him for any metals discovered, to any quarries or mines established, and neither had he the right to timber or 'great trees now growing'. And if the Earl of Hertford's surveyors came to the manor, they were to be provided with food and lodging.

It is apparent that at the time of this lease, Monkton manor had acquired a prosperous range of buildings. How had these originated? The Seymour estate may have constructed a house for their chief tenant, Richard Apharry, who later became a rent collector for the estate. Or perhaps he himself had built a house on the site of the original dwelling of Farleigh Priory's bailiff. The coming of Robert Dyrdo, the Pleydells and William Bayliffe as manor lords is likely to have prompted the building of a larger and more elaborate house than that needed by Richard Apharry. During this time the common fields were being enclosed, and the manor house at Monkton also became the farmhouse for the land around it. The new farming methods called for more buildings, and a prosperous family such as the Bayliffes required extra outbuildings, for such farming needs as cheesemaking and pig rearing, and for the household tasks of brewing, meat and bacon salting, and laundering.

The manor house itself was probably constructed of timbered wattle and daub walls, with a thatched roof, similar to one built by the river at Chippenham in 1584. Since the enclosures, woodland had diminished around the town, thus timber for building was getting scarce. It is not long after that houses in the area began to be built of stone, and Cocklebury farmhouse is likely to have been the first stone dwelling there. Like the Bayliffes, the Goldney family at Cocklebury were probably also living in a timbered dwelling at the end of the 16th century. They had come to Cocklebury and built their house on the site of Rawlings farmhouse at the beginning of the century, before stone houses were constructed in the area.

It is not difficult to trace how the family came to Cocklebury. A John Goldney is first recorded as understeward for the manor of Sheldon in

1486. Thirty years later, with Martin Fleming, a Castle Coombe clothier, he is recorded in Feet of Fines as buying for 200 marks 'lands in Coculborowe, Rawlynges, Langlay Byrrell, and Chippenham'. Previously, Nicholas, John's son, had rented land from Farleigh Priory in 1508 and the leases continued until the Dissolution. He rented Mancroft and the other fields, and had the right to run 100 sheep and 10 'hedd of beaste' on common land there. It may be no coincidence that, a few months before Nicholas obtained his lease, his brother Henry became Rector of Monkton Farleigh and Box, positions over which the Prior of Farleigh had jurisdiction. Henry (Clericus) was involved with Nicholas in several land acquisitions, all Farleigh property, including purchase of land near Thornhill in Langley Burrell. In 1524 he bought land at Tytherton Lucas, near Stanley, belonging to Bradenstoke Priory, evidently to retire to, for he died there five years later.

The Goldney family, besides farming and owning land at Cocklebury for nearly two centuries, were prominent in the woollen industry and played an important role in the municipal affairs of Chippenham. Henry, Nicholas's son, became the first Bailiff (mayor) following the granting of a charter to the town in 1554. It was Henry who was instrumental in bringing to Cocklebury the Scotts, the family of clothiers whose fortunes became closely bound to the Goldneys. Feet of Fines for 1552 records 'Henry Bulle, John Smythe, Thomas Skotte and Agnes his wife, Henry Farnewell alias Goldeney, and John Skott and Matilda his wife' claimed 'messuages and lands in Chipham, Cokylborough, and Langley Burrell'. The Scotts had leased from the Goldneys the old fulling mill at Stanley two years before they bought their land at Cocklebury. The Scott farm there was around Manscroft field, sandwiched between Goldney and Monkton manor land. Until the late 19th century, the field name 'Scots Ground' identified the site of the Scott farmhouse and out-buildings, and traces of the foundations of these buildings were still visible when the author worked at Cocklebury during the Second World War.

There were other families living at Cocklebury in the 16th century, in the Pew Hill area and all along Cocklebury lane and the track to Monkton House. The records are sparse, so little more than their names is known until the next century. The Bakers and Westfields rented land from Monkton manor for 200 years, as did the Gales and the Neates. The Paynes continued their association with Cocklebury, at the same time playing a leading role in public affairs in Chippenham. The Olivers, like the Paynes, had survived the Black Death, and in 1575 Edith Oliver of Cocklebury, a widow, donated lands to Langley Burrell parish in return for prayers to be said at the village church.

The change from monastic to secular ownership at Cocklebury in the first half of the 16th century provided the opportunity to reorganise tenancies and to enclose the open common fields that made up three-quarters of the acreage of Cocklebury. By this time the existing agrarian system no doubt appeared to the new landlards a wasteful way of farming, utilizing neither man, beast or land prudently. Cattle had to be kept from arable crops until their harvesting; grazing rights on pasture and meadows had become a mass of complications over the years; cross ploughing was difficult on the narrow strips and so prevented sufficient aeration of the soils; and drainage was a chronic problem. The system of land division between tenants, however, was the chief barrier to more efficient farming.

The open fields were rented in strips or sections, and one man's land would not necessarily be all together. He could farm a strip or section in one end of a common field, and another a quarter of a mile away. Nicholas Goldney held his arable and pasture land in 1519 among five different common fields—at Cocklebury, Stanley, Sheldon, Lowden and Chippenham—while Richard Apharry in 1532 had no less than 12 sections of land, mostly scattered at Cocklebury. He also held several of the old medieval fields including Matford and part of Mancroft, those in possession of the de Cockleburys and other families until the Black Death.

Thus new fields were formed by the new landlords at Cocklebury, who enclosed small convenient areas with hedges, and centrally located new farmhouses and buildings in a chosen group of fields. It was literally a rearrangement of the land, to create what is considered today a farm. It is interesting to note that until the time of the Tudors the word 'farm' signified a lease or a rent, and was used as a noun, never as a verb.

At Rawlings, the common fields area around the site of the farmhouse today was split up into small fields of ten acres or less and hedged. The Scott land probably remained the same, for it lay in the area of the old small holders' fields. Monkton manor formed a farm around the present site of Cocklebury farmhouse, and created smaller farms around Pew Hill and on the land between the hill and the manor house. The remainder of Cocklebury, except for one common field was attached to the manor as its home farm, much of it the grazing lands along the River Avon.

The term farmer had yet to be used. With the exception of the Bayliffes, who considered themselves gentlemen, the men who managed or who worked the farms at Cocklebury called themselves husbandmen or yeomen. Often, a man, if his farm was small, would have another trade, but he invariably chose to call himself by either of these two titles. Even the more prosperous clothiers of the Goldney family called themselves yeomen for several generations, until their farm at Cocklebury became a secondary part of their lives.

The enclosure of the common fields at Cocklebury took place gradually through the 16th century, apparently with the agreement of the existing tenants, for most remained on the Monkton rent rolls all through the century. There is no evidence that the labourers working at Cocklebury before the Reformation were displaced; probably they continued to be employed by the Bayliffe, Scott and Goldney families, and by the new tenant farmers acquired by the manor.

In some parts of England, however, particularly where the land was mostly arable, the post-Reformation landlords had no hesitation in displacing their labourers and small holders. They either would be given other land (rarely of the same acreage or agricultural value) to work, or would be told to leave and find a living elsewhere. If there was no work in the vicinity, a man with luck might find a small piece of waste or unused land, attempt to build a rough dwelling there between sunset and sunrise, and become a squatter. The agricultural worker at Cocklebury is likely to have been better off than others in many parts of England, for at the time he was needed there. The new agrarian methods were to create a more intensive way of farming and require a plentiful supply of labour before they became fully established. Also, his family had probably worked on the land at Cocklebury for several generations (perhaps, in the case of some families, since the Black Death), and so his knowledge of the area would be of great value towards the work of enclosure of the common fields.

During the years of enclosure, the choice was made at Cocklebury and throughout the Vale to put much of the arable land to pasture (a choice that has been retained to this day), so dairy herds and beef cattle became all-important. A certain amount of cereal and other arable crops were still grown for stock feeding and for human consumption, but later, due to increased cropping and better transportation, cereals for bread and flour were imported into the Vale from other areas, which released even more land for grazing cattle.

The advantages of enclosed fields were many. No unproductive labour was needed to keep the cattle from straying, a constant event in the days of common fields. The cattle could be grazed in a field for a certain period and then moved to eliminate the danger of over-cropping the grass. A field could lie undisturbed to produce grass for haymaking. Enclosed fields segregated cattle and thus ended indiscriminate breeding so stock could be improved. The spread of animal disease could also be controlled to some extent by isolating affected cattle.

To provide water for the animals in the new fields, ponds were dug where they did not already conveniently exist. The clay underlying the sandy loams at Cocklebury was ideal for pond making, for it sealed in the water, preventing seepage and loss of water through the subsoils. Most of the ponds that survived into the 20th century were created for the new fields. One, however, because of its size, and its position by an old settlement area and the common field around the site of Rawlings farmhouse, is likely to have been a relic of medieval times.

At first many of the pastures were semi-permanent; that is, they were ploughed every few years and reseeded. But in time, permanent leys were created, a difficult skill at which farmers of the Vale learnt to excel, and of which they were justly proud in later centuries. The soils and climate of Cocklebury and the Vale were found to be ideally suited to the new pastoral farming. The mild weather, shelter from the winds, and the inevitable rain extended the growing season in the pastures and meadows and provided a heavy crop of hay. The cattle generally wintered out. During the time of little or no growth of grass, between December and March, their diet would be mainly hay, with supplements of oats or barley. As far as is known, root crops such as turnips were not grown in the Vale for cattle food until the 18th century or just before.

Although the number of cattle and pigs increased at Cocklebury after the enclosures, sheep continued to be important animals; valued, however, more for their meat and manure than for their wool. Beef cattle were sent to local market, or joined animals being driven along drovers' routes to London. A small amount of milk from the dairy cows was used for household consumption and to make butter, but the bulk of it went into cheese-making. The manufacture of cheese was to become very important to the economy of the district, especially as later it was made all the year round, thanks to the new farming methods which produced enough hay to feed and to keep many of the cows in milk through the winter. The 16th century can perhaps be considered the start of the cheese and bacon industries around Chippenham. The production of cheese had to be confined to the farmhouse, because of the difficulty of transporting large quantities of milk, but some bacon curing probably took place in the town, for there is mention of a 'bacon-house' there in the 17th century.

The increase in stock, and the extra care needed to maintain the new fields (manuring, hedging, ditching, and draining), meant more labour was needed on the land. Despite views to the contrary, it is likely that the enclosures and the new farming methods in the Vale provided more employment for men and women labourers, rather than less. The 16th century and the beginning years of the 17th, was evidently a period of strong economic growth at Cocklebury and other parts of the Vale. But people's working ways were changing, as was the landscape of the countryside they worked in. What did not change, however, was a person's sense of identity.

As a community, or to be more exact, several communities within one area, Cocklebury had existed for at least 700 years by 1600. Despite new ownership, changing agrarian practices and the economic growth of the woollen industry in the surrounding area, the people of Cocklebury seem to have held onto their tradition of maintaining an identity separate and independent from Chippenham and Langley Burrell. This aspect of their lives did not change, neither did community sentiment in other similar nearby communities such as Fogamshire and Pewsham. Such feelings were to persist until the end of the 19th century; then better communications and a wider view of life destroyed the special involvement local people had with one another. At that time, their sense of community was transferred to the town of Chippenham.

Chapter Six

The 1600s: Social and Economic Change at Cocklebury

In 1600, a person standing in the centre of Cocklebury would be surrounded by neatly-hedged fields with farmhouses interspersed between them. To the east, he would enjoy almost the same view as today: the partially-wooded slope of the Vale's edge, with a glimpse of the Wiltshire Downs behind. To the south, he would see the grazing lands of Cocklebury by the River Avon, and Monkton House–the largest dwelling in the area–surrounded by outbuildings and gardens. There was nothing then to obstruct the view of the Avon flowing gently by Chippenham, and the parish church with its squat tower and spire. Most of the houses of the town could also be seen nestled on the slopes beyond the river bank. Looking westwards, the toll gates at Chippenham Clift and Lands End would be visible over the remaining common field area of Cocklebury, while around Rawlings to the north, the newly-enclosed fields provided a gentle setting for the farmhouse. On Cocklebury Common, cattle would be grazing, to be taken to the nearby pound if they strayed, and held until their owners paid the small fine necessary for their release.

Besides Monkton House and the farmhouses of Cocklebury, there were other dwellings, the homes of small farmers, craftsmen and labourers. They were constructed of materials obtained locally, and remained subsidiary to the countryside. In the 17th century it was the land and its produce that were all-important. Buildings (and the needs of the people living in them) were secondary. Today, modern structures of alien concrete, brick and metal at Cocklebury have almost totally changed the face of its previous landscape, a symbol of man's broken links with the soil that once nurtured him.

In this setting at Cocklebury lived members of a social order or rural class system that was to prevail there for nearly 300 years. At the top was the Bayliffe family, the lords of Monkton manor; then came the Goldneys and the Scott families; next the yeomen farmers, tenants of the manor; at the bottom of the hierarchy were the craftsmen and labourers, whose work was closely linked with either the land or the people of the area. All had their place and a share in the fabric of society there. The size of each individual's share might vary slightly over the years, depending on the ability of each person and general economic prosperity, but a person's position in this rural community seldom altered. A master remained a master, a servant a servant. To better himself, a man would have to move away and learn a new skill; a woman could only hope to do so by marrying into a higher class—not easily done in a small community at that time.

The lord of a small manor in the 17th century had a great deal of power. He was, in some ways, similar to a king in a small kingdom. He knew all his tenants, their families, and the workers on the manor; he controlled the income of his tenants by the amount of rent they had to pay to the manor; very often he influenced the political and religious leanings of the manor's people. In lieu of the Seymour family, the Bayliffes fulfilled the role of manor lord at Monkton and Cocklebury. They supervised the leasing and the husbandry of the manor land to keep it in good heart, presided over the manor court, and maintained a harmonious relationship between the manor and its tenants.

It will be recalled that William, the first Bayliffe at Monkton, had established his family there in the 1560s. Besides being a well-to-do lawyer of Middle Temple, William Bayliffe, by taking the responsibility of the tenancy of the manor, had also selected a way, not unusual for the time, to become a country gentleman. The Bayliffe name soon appeared with the names of other leading local families, and William, while serving as a Burgess (Councilman) of Chippenham, emerged as a well-known figure in the area. But it was his eldest son, Henry, born soon after the family came to Monkton, who was to be the most prominent of all the Bayliffes.

Like his father, Henry was a Middle Temple Lawyer; he was also a Justice of the Peace and a frequent office holder in the government of Chippenham. He counselled the town on legal matters; in 1609, according to municipal records, he gave 'advise and direction about Assarte lands'. For payment, he was given 'a pottle of seck and a lb of sugar and woulde take noe other ffee'. After the death of his father, Henry moved to Monkton from a house in St Mary Street, just across the river at Chippenham.[1]

Following his father's lead, he continued to purchase small parcels of land around Cocklebury, chiefly belonging to Langley manor. This was made possible by the changing state of the affairs of the manor in the first half of the 17th century. The manor, owned by the Berkeley family since the 14th century, had been acquired by two local personages, Edward Reade and Henry White. They formed a shaky partnership, however, and finally in 1657 the manor was purchased by a Somerset clothier, Samuel Ashe. (The manor is retained by the same family today.) Both William and Henry Bayliffe, as close neighbours and witnesses to various deeds of sale and mortgages, had ample opportunity to acquire land near Monkton, and in time they had formed a modest estate, to be conveniently administered with the Monkton manor lands.

During Henry Bayliffe's lifetime, defiance of the monarchy and Puritanism began to emerge in this corner of Wiltshire, as they did in many other parts of England. By the start of the Civil War, the sympathies of the people of Chippenham were for the Parliamentarians, whereas the local gentry were evenly divided between King and Cromwell. Henry sat at Sessions hearing cases against recusants and those who broke laws. No other Justices attended as many as he. It is possible that this indicates a Puritan attitude.

It is interesting to consider how Henry Bayliffe journeyed about. According to the family's Probate Inventories, they did not own any kind of carriage or coach. This was not unusual, for at the time only the very rich could afford such vehicles. For most people in the 17th century, all journeys, long or short, were made by horsebck or pillion, or on foot. The poor state of the roads, and the lack of stopping places along them, prevented anyone from attempting a long journey, unless one of acute necessity. So Henry no doubt went on horseback to special Sessions at Corsham, Calne and Monkton Farleigh, and probably chose to stay overnight at the last named rather than attempt the 17 mile ride back in the dark. To attend to those in Chippenham, he is likely to have taken the family boat from the little dock at Monkton House to cross the river, and then walked up the Common Slip into St Mary Street and the town.

There is very little mention of any activities of the Bayliffes during the Civil War years, and they did not apparently play a prominent role in the troubles besetting Chippenham during that time. This may be because soon after the war began Henry died, and his son William came to Monkton in 1643. William's wife, Elizabeth Norborne, was the daughter of a prominent Chippenham lawyer. Elizabeth is one of the few women who emerge as inidividuals in the Cocklebury story. She was intelligent and capable, a person of rare initiative, and played an active role in solving, besides her own, the problems of other family members living nearby. Her life at the manor lasted for over 60 years. During that time her husband and son died, and the manor was sold by the Seymours, but she lived on at Monkton House, looking after the Bayliffe estate until her death in 1705.

After the Bayliffes, the next in rank in the rural hierarchy at Cocklebury were the Goldneys and Scotts. The similarity of these families to each other is striking. Their connection with Chippenham began at Cocklebury, for 200 years they were both among the leading clothiers of the district, and their fortunes waxed and waned together. Both families branched into two main lines, seemingly with cousins or brothers as respective heads. Scotts and Goldneys intermarried, and to further confuse any historian or genealogist, members of the same generation of different family lines often bore the same Christian names.

Members of both the families were active in borough affairs. To read the Chippenham municipal records of the 17th century is to gain the impression that the Scotts and the Goldneys, along with other clothiers such as the Hawkins and Staffords, the local gentry, and other leading merchants, ran the town as if it were a private club. Their offices passed from father to son, brother to cousin. They ran the town well, and gave Chippenham their loyal and devoted service over many decades. The continuity of government they bestowed on the town helped to maintain its stability, especially at times when the fluctuations caused by the shifting international market greatly affected the prosperity of the local cloth industry.

As Chippenham flourished, so in turn did Cocklebury. Not only by reason of the more intensive agriculture in practice there, but also because the Scotts and the Goldneys invested money in their farms and provided for persons living around the farms, cottage work, such as carding, spinning and weaving. Cocklebury's connection to the woollen industry was being maintained. It had been in existence for more than a century, for Nicholas Goldney had grazed his sheep there as far back as 1509, and there were two fulling mills, Stanley and Scotts, just across the river. Stanley, it will be remembered, had been a fulling mill as far back as 1189.

Both the Goldneys and the Scotts were involved in the processes of cloth making from the fleece to the woven piece. At this time, Chippenham was famous for its broadcloths, and this type of cloth had to be made from wool from sheep that were grazed on high ground. Wool from local sheep accustomed to the wet, comparatively milder climate of the Vale was not, apparently, suitable. To purchase the wool needed, the clothiers or their agents had to travel to markets as far away as the Cotswolds or southern Wiltshire, and the fleeces were brought back to Chippenham by pack horses.

The fleeces would first be sorted and cleaned, then washed and oiled. At first, for close supervision of this important phase of cloth making, the Scotts and Goldneys may have had it done on their premises at Cocklebury. However, as the volume of business increased later in the 17th century, in all likelihood these processes were moved into Chippenham. The wool was then distributed to women, who, in their homes, carded and spun it into yarn. Weavers took this yarn to make into pieces of cloth of specific width and length–hence the name broadcloth. The cloth was then sent to a mill to go through the processes of scouring, fulling and stretching on racks (this is the origin of the name of Rack Close at Chippenham). The resulting broadcloth, after being dyed and dressed elsewhere, was sent by pack horse or carrier's wagons to be sold by the clothiers themselves or by their agents at Blackwell Hall in London.

Until the 18th century it was customary not only for the carding and spinning to be done in the workers' homes, but usually the weaving too. For those living at Cocklebury, engaged in farm work, the outwork of carding and spinning represented extra family earnings. For others completely dependent on it for a living, there was hardship in times of slump in the woollen industry. The records of the 17th century Quarter Sessions, the Poor Law Overseers, and petitions from workers to various authorities testify to this. There is little doubt, however, that the weavers and other workers of the woollen industry at Cocklebury were better off than those living in the town, for there would always be the food they had grown in their own gardens, or that they obtained from the farmers in return for extra work.

Many wills and probate inventories of the Goldney family survive. From them, the men of the family emerge as prosperous solid citizens, perhaps a little uninteresting as personalities, but with affection for their wives and children, respect for other family members, and responsible for those who served them. In 1684 Henry Goldney, the owner of Rawlings, made his will. He left lands, capital and 'my warping barr and all other utensills belonging to the trade of clothing' to his eldest son. He was generous to his other children and to 'the child my wife now goes with' for each were to receive £350, a large dowry for a girl, and enough for a young man with good family trade connections to become a clothier. If the girl did not marry, the sum was still enough to give her independence if she had a family roof over her head. This is what actually happened, for Sarah and Ann, Henry's daughters, were still unmarried 20 years later, and living in one of the Goldney houses in Chippenham. The unborn child, christened Edward, became a clothier in Bristol. As did so many others of his position in life, in his will Henry Goldney distributed his silver tankards amongst his family. His eldest son was bequeathed the best; Gabriell, the next son, the second best; his wife Ann, the third best; and the youngest son, John, the fourth best. Money was left to ensure John's education. Perhaps he attended Mr. Brazier's small private tutorial school, already in existence in Chippenham at the time the will was made.

After farming at Cocklebury for many years, the Goldney family rented Monkton manor land in St Mary Street, where they built their home. It is not clear, however, when the family installed a tenant at Rawlings, and ceased to live there themselves. In the 1700s, the fortunes of the Goldney clothiers declined. Some of the family left Chippenham, and Rawlings was sold. But that is a story belonging to the next chapter of this book.

The involvement of the Scott family in the woollen industry at Chippenham also ended in the 1700s, but a little later than that of the Goldneys. One branch of the Scott family had their farm at Cocklebury, the other at Lowden. There exists a very detailed probate inventory dated 1683 of Jonathan Scott of Chippenham parish. From it the impression is gained that this orderly prosperous family lived in a large farmhouse, very similar in design and age to that of Cocklebury farmhouse. Jonathan's house had two floors and an attic. A hall, parlour and kitchen made up the principle rooms downstairs, with the addition of two butteries behind the kitchen. Either attached to the house, or as separate but conveniently located outhouses, were a brewhouse and a 'whitehouse', the latter was used for washing clothes and for storing linen.[2] The first floor of the house consisted of three rooms, an additional parlour or sitting room, and two bedrooms, each with two beds. The rooms on both floors opened out from one another, so there was very little privacy. There may have been a back staircase or ladder to ensure access into the attic, for this was divided into a loft for cheese storage, and a garret providing sleeping quarters for maid servants.

The contents of these rooms indicate that the Scotts lived a comfortable life; few stools and many leather chairs; both table and sideboards in the living rooms; a kitchen well equipped with pewter and brass utensils; a press and two chests, a desk, a trunk and a box in the biggest bedchamber. Considering the time, and Jonathan's station in life, the house was extremely well furnished. The inventory was held in March, but there was still a large store of wood for the fires, valued at £2 10s, the yearly wage of a dairymaid. As it is rare for any kind of firing to be listed in probate inventories in the same locality, this large amount may have been recorded because it was so unusual. Jonathan's silver plate and money were valued at £300, his farm animals, including six oxen at £150. In his will, he had specified that his eldest son was to inherit £500, and the great press in the bedchamber. He requested him to help Elizabeth, his wife, to sell his stock of cloths and other goods. Obviously Elizabeth Scott, besides running a house, was expected by her husband to manage his business affairs after his death.

As the leading families prospered at Cocklebury during the 17th century, so did the small farmers. The increase in their standard of living was partly due to their security of tenure and low rents, partly due to their own investments in their farms, and partly to the increase in the general economy of the countryside. Most leases ran for three lives, from grandfather to grandson, and usually were renewed to the same family if they wished to stay. Knowing he was going to remain on the same land, a yeoman was willing to put a small percentage of his monetary income into the farm as capital expenditure and, as a result, gradually increase its yields. He might consider expanding his dairy herd in order to make more cheese. Or he might buy a piece of equipment, such as a roller or another

1. Sir Edward Seymour, afterwards first Duke of Somerset, who acquired much of the land at Cocklebury after the Dissolution of the Monasteries. (*From* The Wardens of Savernake Forest, *by the Earl of Cardigan, Routledge & Paul, reproduced with permission*)

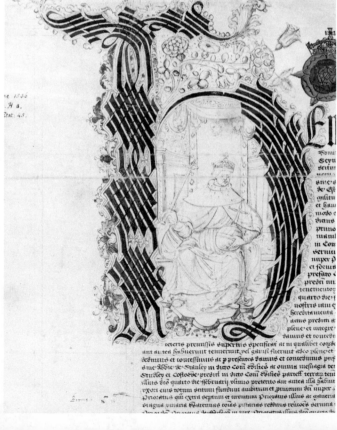

2. The gold, red and blue illuminated letter depicting Henry VIII, from the manuscript granting Seymour lands in Wiltshire, including Cocklebury. (*Reproduced by permission of the Trustees of the Pierpoint Morgan Library*)

3. (*left*) Monkton House and its walled garden, 1710. (*From Chippenham in Bygone Days by George White, and reproduced with permission*)

4. (*above*) Hardenhuish House.

5. (*below*) Monkton House 1919. Both Hardenhuish and Monkton were probably built by John Wood & Sons, the famous Bath architects, between 1774 and 1780.

6a. & b. (*above*) Top: the original bridge carrying the Calne line over the River Avon at Cocklebury, built 1863. Bottom: the steel bridge which replaced the original one, known locally as the 'Black Bridge'. (*Reproduced by permission from* The Calne Line *by G. Tanner, 1972*)

7. (*right*) Making a cutting on the Great Western Railway; how the scene at Cocklebury would have appeared. (*Reproduced by permission of the Science Museum, London*)

8. (*below*) The railway cutting at Cocklebury today.

9. This chimney is a relic of one of several metal workshops that sprang up around Foundry Lane after the coming of the Great Western Railway.

10. Cocklebury Farm and outbuildings (including 18th-century barn on right) in 1919, at the time of the sale to Charles Tucker.

11. Maud Tucker (right) and friends outside Cocklebury farmhouse in 1923. Note stones from cider mill.

12. The Chippenham Depot of the Wiltshire Creameries Ltd., 1924. Milk from Cocklebury was delivered here by horse and wagon for over 50 years. (*From* Rural Life in Wessex *by J. H. Bettey, and reproduced by permission*)

13. Gordon Self in the exact replica in miniature of a Wiltshire farm wagon, still in the Self family's possession. The driver was four years old, the donkey 40 and the passengers four months.

14. Time out from work: the author (left) and cousin riding at Cocklebury.

15. (*above*) Peggy Self with pupil and horses from Cocklebury riding school. Note roofs of stable and cowshed.

16. (*left*) Charlie Gullis the carter observes two minutes silence at the end of World War Two (11 November 1945) with his two horses, Bonnie and Blackie.

17. View of Monkton across
the River Avon, 1948.

18. The same view in 1983
with the houses of Monkton
estate.

19. Aerial view of Cocklebury and Monkton in 1949. (*Crown Copyright, R.A.F. photograph*)

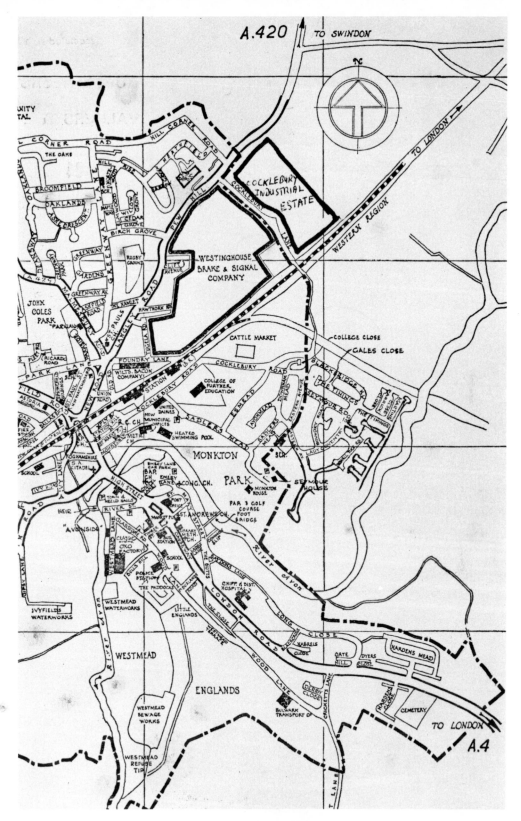

20. This map illustrates the extent of the building at Cocklebury and Monkton (the curve of the river can be used for comparing the two illustrations). (*Reproduced by permission*)

21. Aerial view of Cocklebury farm, 1960.

22. Gordon and Peggy Self (the former on a 19th-century tricycle) in front of the old farm buildings.

23. The calf sheds built to replace the old farm buildings.

24. (*above*) Mr. E. A. Self with the Cocklebury pedigree Friesian herd in the mid-1950s.
Note the elms in the hedgerows.

25. (*right*) Mr. Self with Gordon and Silver
Duke, the foundation bull of the Cocklebury
herd.

26. Silver Dolly, highest yielding cow of the Cocklebury
herd.

27. Cocklebury farmhouse, 1983.

28. The start of the Cocklebury Industrial Estate, 1981.

29. Part of the Monkton hous-
ing estate, looking towards the
Westinghouse Brake and Signal
Company Ltd.

wagon, for even as far back as the 17th century the pleasure of purchasing new machinery existed for farmers! Several wills and inventories of yeomen farming in the Cocklebury area have survived, but a description of them all would overwhelm the reader with detail. Here are three that supply a considerable amount of information on life there in the 17th century: the wills of Gabriel Baker,[3] Nicholas Gale and Robert Gale.

In 1646 Gabriel Baker of Cocklebury, a widower, died after a long illness. He described himself as being 'sick and sorely wounded, but in sound and perfet mind and memorie, Thank God'. The wording of the will creates an impression that Gabriel was either a very pious man, or wished to make sure that he was going to meet his maker, for his religious sentiments are emphatically stated. He had five children, three sons and two daughters. In his will he left the two younger sons, Richard and Thomas, £10 and £5 respectively. Marie, his elder daughter, was bequeathed £15, a yearling colt, several pieces of furniture including a bedstead with its featherbed, and her mother's best gowns and petticoats. The younger daughter, Ann, who was willed 10s to buy a mourning ring, also received a featherbed, and a chest. But Gabriel owed Ann £10 and instructed that she be paid double that amount within two years of his death. An intriguing debt. Both bequests to the daughters are obviously meant to provide a small dowry if either married. Gabriel knew that the estate would be short of ready money to pay the debt to Ann immediately after his death; he arranged repayment so that any suitor would be assured of an eventual marriage portion. Gabriel's eldest son, Robert, received 'all the rest of my goods, chattels, household stuff, utensills, implements of household moveable and immoveable, be not herein before given or bequeathed'. Two friends were left his best and second best suits of leather. His attendant Joan Gale inherited 10s, as did his maid Susan. The two servant boys each received five shillings. Witnesses to the will were members of two well-known families of Langley Burrell, the Alands and the Effingtons.

Another yeoman, Nicholas Gale, living near Cocklebury, died in 1617. He evidently had retired from farming, for although farm implements are listed in his inventory, there are no animals, except for a mare and her colt and one heifer. The house Nicholas lived in was small, a combined parlour and kitchen on the ground floor and a bed chamber above. Attached outhouses held equipment for brewing, baking, and salting meat. There is also mention of a reel for yarn, so someone in the household either spun for themselves, or at one time had taken in yarn for spinning from one of the local clothiers. This was an early inventory of the century; those made towards the end indicate that by then meat salting and brewing were no longer so frequently carried out in the home.

Robert, another member of the Gale family, died in 1675. The animals and equipment he left provide a clear picture of the stock of a small farm at Cocklebury at that time. He worked the land with a yoke of oxen, and three horses. The stock consisted of 11 kine (milking cows), six young 'beefs', a bull, 29 sheep and three pigs. The horses were used to pull his wagon and the 'dung pott', a two-wheeled cart to take manure to the fields (a task the author frequently did at Cocklebury in the 1940s), and to harrow his fields. No equipment for working the oxen is recorded, only their yoke and chain. The inventory was taken in November, so the stock of winter feed was almost untouched. It consisted of oats and rye, but chiefly hay. The amount was stated as 25 wagon loads, surely proof of the ability of Cocklebury fields to produce good hay crops. The rakes, pitch forks, scythes, flails and many other work tools needed to accomplish the numerous tasks of the farm through the seasons seldom appeared on a farmer's inventory, as it was customary for a worker to supply his own implements unless he lived at the farmhouse. Robert Gale's house was not that much bigger than that of Nicholas Gale. The living and cooking area consisted of one room; behind it was the usual buttery and whitehouse. A chamber over the hall provided a sleeping room with three beds, and a room over the buttery held five hundredweights of cheese, and 'other lumber goods'. This phrase is frequently used in inventories. It covered items of too low a value to be listed individually, and no doubt the discarded items of farms and households always present through the ages in all but the very poorest of societies.

The contrast of wealth at Cocklebury is revealed by this will and others. Henry Goldney was able to leave each of his five children £350. Elizabeth Bayliffe of Monkton at her death in 1705 had over £700 in securities, debts owed to her and ready money. But most craftsmen and labourers at Cocklebury did not have £5-worth of worldly goods to justify a will or a probate inventory.

From leases and mortgages it can be ascertained that at this time there were many small houses at Cocklebury inhabited by workers. Some were documented as tenants with 'messuage and garden', this phrase inferring a better home than that of the unskilled worker. Although both craftsmen and laboureres comprised the working class at Cocklebury, they in turn had their hierarchy, based upon skills. Their top ranks included the carpenters, masons, and thatchers employed by the manor and the farmers to build and repair houses and out buildings. In these ranks too would be found the weavers, fullers and other skilled artisans of the woollen industry.

Labourers on the farms at Cocklebury followed a variety of skills, many of which had not changed for centuries, and were not to change until mechanisation came to the farm. Ploughman, hedger and ditcher, horseman or carter, pigman, shepherd, milker and dairymaid, mower and reaper, each man or woman had a particular occupation. On smaller farms at Cocklebury, labourers would perform two or more skills, the shepherd shearing his sheep, the ploughman serving as carter and horseman, but their work remained confined to related skills.

At this time formal education was seldom provided for the children of these workers. Instead a child acquired his parent's skill for his education, by working at his side. In turn, he as a parent would pass his skill on to his children, forming a chain of knowledge often not broken until the 20th century when his skill was either replaced by a mechanical tool, or abandoned as too expensive to use.

Finally at Cocklebury there were labourers and servants needed to perform the routine unskilled work, the periodic cleaning of the cattleyards and pigsties, manure spreading, thistle and nettle cutting, and the domestic work of the farmhouses. These men and women hired for the outside work earned less than 1s a day. And for a few pence, their wives, helped by young children, hoed and weeded the arable crops, picked the apples and pears for cider and perry, and did other seasonal jobs. The domestic workers were usually hired on a yearly basis for £1 or so, and lived in the farmhouse.

By the standards of the times, these labourers and their families were well off until the middle of the century, for there were still many workers in England who were frequently unemployed or itinerant. Towards the end of the century, however, prices began to rise. Wages remained at about the same level, hence the purchasing power of the labourer began to decrease. As there was still a surplus of labour, the farmer had no need to increase wages to compensate for higher prices. By 1700 the custom of low wages for the agricultural worker had begun, and was to continue until after the Second World War. In a small society such as Cocklebury, diminishing wages also meant that the gap between the rich and the poor was to increase, the labourer becoming more dependent on his employer. But at least his job was secure, and he had a permanent roof over his head.

That roof may only have covered one or two crude rooms, but by the end of the century, improvement had come to labourers' homes, as it had to those of other classes. The walls of clay were strengthened with timber to make them more durable. Dirt floors were exchanged for flagstone; shutters discarded for glass windows; a fireplace and chimney replaced the central fire, with its smoke formerly filling the room and only gradually seeping out from a hole through the thatch. 'Outshuts'–extra lean-to rooms–were often added onto the main wall to serve as an extra sleeping room, a larder, or a shelter for a pig or cow, relieving the cramped living quarters of the inevitable large family. Despite the improvements, very few dwellings such as these without stone foundations or walls survive from the 17th century. None do at Cocklebury–not even a trace of them. The oldest remaining cottage there today, built of rough stone and rubble, dates from around the end of the 18th century.

Women's work at Cocklebury never ceased. Probably only Bayliffe women were able to enjoy any leisure time. The others, even if they had servants to do the hard manual work, had to supervise such important farm tasks as butter and cheese making, the salting and smoking of meat and bacon, the bee-keeping and the growing of fruits, vegetables and herbs. All these tasks were vitally important, for if done incorrectly, part of the winter food supply would be irrevocably lost, and impossible to replace until the following year.

Bearing in mind that towards the end of the century there was a little more cash income for the farmer, such goods as soap, candles, and cloth were no doubt purchased in Chippenham, thus relieving the women of the arduous work of making them. The extra money also provided furniture and utensils for the household, and for a greater variety of food, which was becoming available because of the improved communications with distant and overseas markets at the time. But such purchases also created more work, so the better living standards obtained were gained at the expense of the women's work and time.

Besides the customary household chores, the carrying of water, cooking, cleaning, scrubbing, the washing of clothes and linen, there were many other jobs always waiting to be done. Meat was purchased in sides and quarters, and had to be cut up before it was cooked. Blocks of salt and sugar needed grinding. Wood had to be chopped for the fire which was always kept burning in the kitchen (coal from Somerset was too expensive for all but the very wealthiest of families). All clothes except those of leather had to be made at home. Butter was churned weekly, more frequently in hot weather. Home remedies and medicines had to be concocted. Except in the driest of months, there was always the wet to cope with. Damp work clothes had to be dried out, and the ever-present muddy clay to be kept out of the house. For the young married woman, beyond all these household duties, there was constant child bearing and raising. So little was ever heard of women in the 17th century, except in the domestic setting, unless she was of the aristocracy or of independent means, for she could never escape from her work and lived her life only through her husband, her children, and her household.

Towards the end of the 17th century, food became a little more plentiful. The old constant fear of famine if a harvest failed had been eradicated by better farming and transportation. If corn or other cereals did become short in the Vale, Somerset or south Wiltshire could now be depended upon to make up the deficiency. The diet of the Vale people varied according to their class, but their basic foods were divers and adequate nutritionally, consisting of rye and barley bread, pease pudding, a little bacon and ham, butter and plenty of cheese. Small birds and rabbits ('connyes' as an old document describes them) could be trapped in nearby burrows and hedgerows, for poaching was not yet considered the serious crime it was to be in later years. Carp, perch, roach, pike and eel were taken from the Avon, but not by 'draught or casting nett'.

Those with gardens were better off. A description of one at Stanley in a 1584 lease describes 'apples plumes, cheryes and other such fruit tree or trees ther growing', and these fruits were dried or otherwise preserved for eating through the year. Cocklebury residents with a small house and garden are likely to have shared brewing, salting and baking facilities, as such an arrangement is described in the above lease.

One of the advantages to living at Cocklebury was its close proximity to Chippenham. It was easy to get cattle and produce to market, and the several roads nearby permitted frequent communication with the town and the outside world. This is not to give the impression that to travel was simple. Except for short distances, it was not. Roads were unpaved routes that ran from town to town, and village to village, and in winter they could widen to many yards in open countryside, in order to avoid areas of mud often several feet deep.

Until the middle of the 17th century, the major form of traffic on these roads was the pack horse. Not being weighty, a pack horse could manage to negotiate all but the muddiest sections of the route. And if the mud was too deep, the horses could always be diverted. Not so for the heavy cumbersome carrier wagons that began to appear at the end of the 16th century. They would often be pulled by oxen, for the cloven hoof of an ox could pull out of much deeper mud that that of a horse. In all but the dry summer months most of the roads on the clay of the Vale must have been a sea of mud, sometimes with a narrow filled-in stone surface in the centre for horses and pedestrians. The muddy section of the London to Bristol road from Pewsham to the top of St Mary Street at Chippenham was notorious for difficulties in negotiating it, despite the causeway built upon it in medieval times, and was a constant cause for complaint.

In 1555, with the realisation that something had to be done about the roads of England, Parliament passed an Act, shifting the responsibility for their maintenance from the manor lords to individual parishes. To fulfil the purpose of the Act, the parishes put men to work on the roads for a few days every year. They provided minimal care; probably only the largest mudholes were filled in with stones and the central track maintained for horses and foot traffic. A century later, roads had improved to the extent that the carrier wagons, at least in the south of England, would make their journeys all the year round, while clumsy unsprung coaches began to carry passengers on the nine major routes out of London, including the road to Bristol.

In 1651, at about the same time as the start of coaching, the parishes of Chippenham, Hardenhuish, and Langley Burrell agreed on the upkeep of the roads that were 'intermix' among the three parishes. There is no doubt that the residents of Cocklebury would have benefited from this agreement, not only for their own local travel, but for persons and carriers journeying to Cocklebury.

After all, there were often travellers on the roads likely to call there, such as peddlers and 'higglers'. A peddler's pack of the times is described as containing 'one piece of stoolework [a small tapestry to work?], five pieces of drawn work of holland cloth, two leather purses, one piece of ribbon, a pack of shoemaker tackle, several girdles [embroidered belts], a knife and a bone comb'. Besides haberdashery, often such packs would contain small amounts of tea, spices, stationery, household remedies and trinkets, all to appeal to the feminine taste. Higglers, travelling dealers of the times, probably called to bargain with a farmer for corn, forage, and cheeses; and with his wife to exchange small commodities, such as peddlers carried, for her poultry, butter and eggs. This farm produce would be collected by the higglers at a central point, and sent to city markets, London and Bristol, for instance. By participating in such dealings, the farmer avoided tolls and a journey to market, while the higgler gained the higher prices of the cities. Certainly these travellers would provide a welcome diversion from everyday toil at Cocklebury, for time would be taken to discuss the news of the day, the state of the crops, and always, it is certain, the weather.

One way for a farmer to get cattle to London markets and better prices was to have his animals join cattle being driven from Wales to London. For at least three centuries, such droving routes had been well established. The nearest to Cocklebury, after crossing the Severn, continued to Calne, and then joined the Berkshire Ridgeway north of Marlborough to lead into London. The drovers bypassed Chippenham to avoid its toll gates, but it would be easy to take cattle from Cocklebury, via Hardenhuish, to join the route at Biddestone, and at the same time avoid the tolls. Drovers also brought pigs from Wales to Wiltshire, to be fattened on local farms with the whey left over from cheese making. As pigs are notoriously difficult to drive, a journey with a number of them, of such a long distance, must have been hard, tiring work trying the patience of any man, however good natured.

Another form of contact with the outside world at Cocklebury in the 17th century was made through letter carriers. These men journeyed the roads by foot and horseback, carrying letters to and from exchange points. A letter from a distance might go through many carriers' hands until it reached Cocklebury, but the service, though slow, was regular and reliable.

Probably the biggest event of the week for those at Cocklebury was the market at Chippenham, easily reached by boat over the Avon at Monkton, or by foot or horseback over the town bridge. By the 1600s Chippenham was well supplied with shops, inns and taverns, so that market day, a Saturday (though in 1652 the Puritans changed the day to Friday, for they considered a market on the day before or after a Sunday was to 'defile the Lord's Day'), attracted people from a radius of at least 10 miles, and filled the town with busy, bustling people, intent on buying and selling, meeting friends and relatives, exchanging gossip, or just enjoying themselves.

The variety of goods on sale reflected the increasing demands of most of the community and their ability to pay for them. But even the poorest could afford such pleasures as spice cakes and buns from the bakers, a tankard of ale, or a little wine from John Bull, a local vintner. The farmers' wives, their daughters or their servants could purchase their food staples–flour, sugar, dried fruit (including prunes, a most popular item at that time), and oil from the 'grosser' shops, and more specialized items such as candles or soap from the tallow chandler and soap maker. Chippenham, as one of the centres of the woollen industry, was well supplied with drapery shops selling, besides haberdashery, ribbons and other small items, various kinds of woollen cloth, and such fabrics as velvet, silk, and lace. The town was also a centre for tanning, and had several establishments selling leather goods, particularly harness for horses and oxen, household needs such as buckets, bed hangings, leather covered chests, and items of clothing–boots, shoes, gloves, jackets and pants.

The heart of the market was the Shambles, an old word meaning a table to display meat. Here butchers, fishmongers, costermongers, poulterers all had their stalls or open shops. In the market place itself were held the sales of cattle, sheep, and perhaps pigs, from nearby farms. Probably there were not too many horse sales, for Devizes was then considered the prime local market for their sale or purchase, as Warminster was for large amounts of grain, the wheat, barley and oats usually grown on the Chalklands. There is no doubt that Chippenham was as famous for its cheese in the 17th century as later, when it became such an important commodity that special markets were held for its sale.

The market was supervised by special appointees from the holder of the market licence, at this time the burgesses of Chippenham. Weights and measures were regularly inspected; there is a record of a Thomas Wood of Cocklebury who in 1607 was brought before the market stewards and fined for failing to bring his weights and measurements to be compared with the standards. Leather was checked for improper tanning, bakers' goods for their correct weight, and meat for its description. For example, mutton could not claim to be lamb or veal. Licences were needed to trade and carry goods to and from the market, or to buy specific commodities in bulk, such as butter, cheese or grain. These licences helped to keep a check on a trader in order to prevent him from 'engrossing', i.e. cornering the market in his particular item, or conspiring to fix prices. This frequently occurred in the early part of the century when poor harvest invariably meant food shortages, and hence profits to be made on scarce items. Later, as the roads improved and wheeled vehicles could move all the year round, grain came into Chippenham from other parts, providing more and even supplies through the year, thus defeating the engrossers.

Farmers (but probably not their wives!) could enjoy the conviviality of the surrounding inns, after their business was done in the Market Place. There were at least a dozen in Chippenham by 1686. On market day, not only did they serve as a drinking and eating place, but as somewhere to collect purchases and accomplish private business. Room would be provided for the offices of the scrivener and the money lender, who also extended bills of exchange and credit. In a limited sense, these men served the same financial purposes as the banks of today.

Besides the weekly market at Chippenham, seasonal fairs were also held, supplying further occasions for sociability while doing business at the same time. A fair day was a public holiday and attracted many more people and traders than the weekly market. There were two hiring fairs, held on Lady Day and Michaelmas Day. They provided the opportunity for farmers to seek and engage farm labourers and servants, while those that needed a job of the same kind would hold a symbol of their trade and wait to be approached. Fairs were times of jollity and entertainment. They offered much food and drink, fortune telling and illegal gambling, cock fights, bull baiting and occasionally bear baiting.[4] But they also attracted petty thieves and pickpockets, and offered various additional ways of cheating the careless or the unobservant.

There were other days that also provided a break from work for the people of Cocklebury. Of course, Christmas and Boxing Day, Easter and Whitsun were holidays, but others included Spring Festival Day, May Day, Midsummer Day, and two celebration days created in the 17th century, Oakapple and Guy Fawkes. Most of these days marked the passing of the seasons, and customary entertainment would be provided, such as plays of the mummers at Christmas, and in the summertime, weather permitting, Morris dancing. Shrove Tuesday was traditionally noisy, a reaction, no doubt, to shriving the previous Saturday. Chippenham municipal records mention a custom not abandoned until 1756, that of 'throwing at cocks' on Shrove Tuesday. There is no specific mention of any of these events occuring at Cocklebury, but they were customary in other parts of Wiltshire and nearby, and can be inferred to have taken place at Cocklebury. A break in routine is always welcome and there was in the 17th century no other way except by these holidays to obtain a pause from work, unless one was too young, too old, too rich, or too sick to work.

Puritanism, which never valued worldly pleasures, at times put its pall on life at Cocklebury. Local cases from the Quarter Sessions records could be cited to support this view, such as the miller living nearby who was informed on for fishing in his own mill pond during the time of prayers at church on Sunday morning. Persecution of witches, complaints of card playing and drunkenness in taverns, and the risk of persecution for nonconformity to the Church of England would tend to threaten peace of mind. A Mrs. Aland was brought to Quarter Sessions for insulting the vicar of Kington St Michael. She also insulted the Justices she appeared before, but her punishment, if any, is not recorded. Curiously enough, the use of tobacco survived Puritanical criticism, perhaps beause it became a source of revenue. Retailers were licensed and there were two in Chippenham in 1637. It was also sold in taverns and inns in small pipefuls. Such clay pipes are still to be picked up occasionally in fields in the area. One at Cocklebury found a few years ago bears the mark of Richard Greenland, a maker at Marlborough or Devizes, around 1650.

How big a part the parish church at Chippenham played in the life of people at Cocklebury is hard to assess. The Bayliffes, Goldneys and Scotts, the Gales and the Bakers were in regular attendance, for their baptisms, marriages and deaths are faithfully recorded. A perusal of the Chippenham parish registers of the 17th century gives the impression that the church was important to them, but whether as an article of faith, habit, or social convention is impossible to assess. All families of the times had many children, and it is striking that so many of them died at birth or in the first few months of their lives. Because of the number of women recorded as dying in childbirth, marriage must have been a frightening step for a young girl.

There is much interesting detail to be gleaned from the registers, as the following examples will show. 'A poor boy dyinge at Cockleborough' was buried in 1631 without even a name. Who was he? Where did he come from? 'Old Margaret Hyll of Cockleborrowe' died in 1628, Edith Hill in 1637 and Robert Hyll 21 years later. Who were the Hill family? Were they related to John Hyll who appeared in a 1524 Feet of Fines deed concerning lands in Langley Burrell? William Iles of Stanley, killed by a soldier soon after the battle of Roundway Down in the Civil War was buried 'ye 17th of July' 1643. A few weeks later, John the son of widow Harris of 'Titherton' was drowned in the river by Cocklebury. Was he her only son and provider? A whole story could no doubt be woven around this simple entry in the register.

The registers also convey the terrible consequences of the plague in the area during the century. By far the worst epidemic occurred in 1611. There were 180 burials at the parish church during the year, of which the vicar succinctly noted 130 were due to plague. Frequently several members of the same family were buried together, and shared the same service. Robert Haymes, his wife Ales (Alice), and their unnamed 'infant newborn' were all interred on 5 July 1611. John Scott lost his wife, three daughters, and a son in the space of two weeks. Henry Payne from Cocklebury was buried in September, and Richard Westfield's wife, son and daughter in the following November. The Burgesses of Chippenham decided that because of the 'great affliction and misery' in the town both poor and rich should be moved to dwell elsewhere. Whether anyone did move is not recorded. Justices of the Peace at the Quarter Sessions agreed through 'meditation and clemency' that they should be 'Christian and commiserate' with the people of the area. The distress of Chippenham became so great that Parliament levied a £40 weekly rate on all towns within a certain radius for their relief. Bradford-on-Avon and Westbury were excluded from the levy as they too were sorely tried by the plague.

From the burial registers during the next 50 years it seems that the plague remained endemic in the area and in other parts of Wiltshire–a frightening threat to live with for so many years. In 1642, the Burgesses ordered a watch for persons travelling from Malmesbury who exhibited symptoms of the plague. The watch was probably kept at the Langley toll gate, and apparently achieved its aim, for there is no evidence that anyone in Chippenham died of the disease that year. In 1658, several persons died at Cocklebury, perhaps indicating the plague or another disease had struck there: Robert Hill, Thomas Aust 'a husbandman from Monkton', widow Wotton, and John Gale 'buried from Sambourne's farms', and a little later in 1659 William Scroff 'from the house of Robert Baker of Cockleborro'. The last plague year at Chippenham and throughout all England–1666–was known as the year of the Great Plague. Though the death rate was not high at Chippenham, Kilvert, the 19th-century diarist of the area, relates the following report passed down through several generations; apparently at Kington St Michael the plague was so devastating that the main street through the village was green with grass for several months as life there came to a halt.

Not only the plague caused distress. Another problem of the times had been forced upon the people of Cocklebury: which side to support in the event of civil war, the monarchy or the Parliamentarians? It is apparent from contemporary documents that by the commencement of war there was strong support for the Parliamentarians in this corner of Wiltshire. John Aubrey remarked that the 'men of the Clays' were melancholy, contemplative and malicious, hence likely to be supportive of religious dissent and Parliamentarianism. It is more likely, however, that a combination of other factors produced this strong support. The self-reliance of the small farmers, prosperous merchants and clothiers is one factor. Another is the presence of textile workers, who for economic reasons were sometimes compelled to petition, riot or otherwise protest against the economic system of the times which they saw as the fault of the King. A third is the lack in north-west Wiltshire of the influence of the great landlords (such as the Pembrokes of the chalk country), who invariably supported the King. These are far more likely to have led to independence of thought and a rejection of the absolutionism of government as propounded by the two Stuart kings, James I and his son Charles.

Whether the Church of England had any influence on the people's choice is difficult to assess. Although they obviously supported their church, leading families in the Chippenham area attempted to remain neutral during the conflict. Later, after the war, non-conformity grew strong in the nearby villages, but in Chippenham it was slow to become established until the beginning of the 19th century. It is the author's opinion that there well may have been a discerning rejection of Puritanism among the rural families of Cocklebury, and a recognition of a less dogmatic and extreme philosophy of life. This in turn could have contributed to a certain contentment with life there before the outbreak of the Civil War.

When the war began in 1642, life became more difficult at Cocklebury, for during the four years of hostilities Chippenham was a troubled area. Being open and defenceless, and a major cross-roads of the region, the town was frequently forced to accommodate troops of both sides. Municipal officials did their best to pursue a neutral policy, but the war years proved anxious times, when it was no doubt only possible to express feelings and opinions behind closed doors, or in places devoid of eavesdroppers.

The people did not always remain silent, however, as the case of Robert Moore reveals. Pressed at Chippenham to serve for the King, he refused. The Royalist Colonel Chester sentenced him to be hanged. Residents of the town offered the Colonel £30 or three men willing to fight on the Royalist side in exchange for his life. The Colonel rejected these offers. Moore still refused to serve the King, and so he was hanged. This case is unusual, for sympathies were publicly admitted, and there is no record in the area of such sympathisers being persecuted by their opponents.

Events before and after the battle of Roundway Down near Devizes in 1643 show how difficult a role Chippenham had to play during the war. Both Royalist and Parliamentarian armies mustered troops for the battle at different ends of the town. After the fighting the victorious Royalists then chased their opponents back through Chippenham to beyond Malmesbury. On this occasion there was much verbal manoeuvering between municipal officials and the Royalist commander for supplies for the army. All through the war commanders of both sides demanded supplies and forage. Adam Goldney, Henry's cousin, was one of the burgesses closely involved with keeping the peace, while trying to get the troops out of the town as soon as possible. These activities no doubt provided much gossip and speculation among Cocklebury residents, but the greatest impact on them occurred in 1645, almost at the end of the war.

There had been a series of local skirmishes during the day. Towards dusk the soldiers clashed in Fogamshire, the Royalists chasing the Parliamentarians up the High Street into St Mary Street. Some of the Parliamentarian troops, driven into the River Avon there, were drowned, but many were taken prisoner or escaped. As their way of escape lay through the fields of Cocklebury, it can be imagined how terrifying this incident must have been to those in their houses there. Their sympathies may well have been for the escaping troops; but how could they give help without fear of reprisals from the Royalist troops? As has always been the tragedy of civil wars, their fear and perhaps refusal to help was directed against a fellow countryman.

Another clue to the conditions at Cocklebury during the Civil War was supplied by the Justices of the Peace and illustrated how difficult it was to obtain supplies or to move animals and produce to market. At one Quarter Sessions in Wiltshire, the Justices considered the roads 'very dangerous to travel, by reason of interruption of the soldiers' and so decided not to fault anyone for non-appearance at the courts. In 1645 Sessions were not held 'for the whole of Wiltshire was up in arms and large bodies of soldiers of both sides were stationed and fighting throughout the country'.

After the war, many men and widows appeared at the Quarter Sessions to request pensions. A local man who fought against the King was Robert Collier of Kington Langley, a carpenter. He served all through the War, up the final battle at Worcester, where he was alongside his brother, who was killed. His appeal for a pension was granted; the Justices gave him £1, and a yearly stipend of £2. Though not a great sum, (less than one-fifth of a labourer's annual wage) this money would almost certainly be supplemented with Robert's earnings from carpentry work.

Times continued to be troublesome for several years after the termination of hostilities. Th broadcloth weavers at Chippenham and Calne in 1647, protesting their 'miserable conditions for want of work', cited one reason: soldiers during the war had slaughtered the sheep, so that there was a lack of fleeces to provide wool for the cloth. There were many ex-soldiers without means wandering around the countryside, and a campaign in Ireland entailed the movement of troops in the county, sometimes through Chippenham. Despite the return of Charles II in 1660, north Wiltshiremen continued their loyalty to the principles of parliamentary government, for the Restoration created little enthusiasm or approval in the area.

Neither did the accession of the pro-Catholic James II, 25 years later. Soon after, in an attempt to assure a Protestant throne in England, Charles II's natural son James, Duke of Monmouth, was encouraged to believe he could be King. Longleat House was one focal point of his support, which spread from there into south Wiltshire and Somerset. Elements of Monmouth's army on three occasions moved through Chippenham on their way to battle, but there is no record of any of his followers coming from the area. Evidently Parliamentarianism was as strong as ever in the Vale. The subsequent defeat of Monmouth, William and Mary's succession to the Throne, and the ensuing Bill of Rights brought about the effective transfer of power from the throne to the Houses of Parliament.

At Cocklebury, the remaining years of the century were to pass without any events of major importance except the change of ownership of Monkton manor. The Goldneys and the Scotts still prospered, the yeomen cultivated their farms, and when employment was available the cloth workers toiled at the riverside mills or within their homes. Little was to change until the next century, when external economic pressures began to alter a style of life that in most instances had been established at Cocklebury as far back as Tudor times.

Chapter Seven

The Eighteenth Century: Prosperity and Progress

The passing of the Bill of Rights in 1689 effectively signalled the end of the struggle between the monarchy and Parliament for political power. The problems of politics and religion were no longer of such immediate concern as in the earlier part of the century, so the people of north-west Wiltshire could turn their attention to their own affairs once more. The economy of the Vale was firmly based on agriculture and the woollen cloth industry. Responding to the demands of growing domestic markets (for England doubled its population to 11 million between 1700 and 1801), farmers slowly increased their production of food, particularly of meat and cheese in the Vale. To expand their farming they needed a larger amount of capital. If this was available, as well as a long lease and a little initiative, the farmers prospered, even if their workers did not. A manufacturer of cloth in the Vale was not always as fortunate as a farmer, however, although his markets too had expanded. The cloth industry, always volatile, began to suffer in the 18th century from the competition of mills in the north of England. During the period of this chapter, the industry had many economic fluctuations, and to stay in business, a clothier had to have not only good business acumen, but also plenty of easily-realised capital to tide him over periods of what is today called recession.

Unfortunately, weavers and other workers in the woollen trade seldom shared the general prosperity of the Vale in the 18th century. Like agricultural workers, they were much worse off by the end of the century than at its beginning, and the first 30 years of the following century were to prove disastrous to them all.

What happened to the economy of Cocklebury and to its people during the period of this chapter can be traced chiefly in three ways. First of all, by land transactions, which were many, and gradually resulted in ownership being consolidated in a few families. Secondly, by the loss, gain or alteration of vernacular buildings, for these can demonstrate the effects of the shifting economy on Cocklebury. But it is by the third method–a study of changing farming methods–that prosperity can be most clearly illustrated. It is fortunate that the 18th century saw a proliferation of writers on agriculture who described English husbandry in minute detail. North-west Wiltshire did not escape their attention. From such authorities as William Marshall and Arthur Young, the gradual growth and changes in farming at Cocklebury can be visualized. The pattern of alteration was hardly perceptible from one decade to another, even from one generation to another. But alter it did, and this chapter is an attempt to determine and describe the changes occurring on the land, and in the lives of the people there.

The first record of change at Cocklebury during the 18th century really begins with a deed of 1682. It concerns a house at Pew Hill and several parcels of adjoining land. The house belonged to Mary Norborne, widow of a prominent Chippenham attorney, and mother of Elizabeth, who had married William Bayliffe of Monkton. The land, mortgaged to Mrs. Norborne, was previously owned by the Bayliffes, and William Bayliffe and Mary Norborne jointly leased the house and the land to William Bedford, a Chippenham ironmonger. He eventually purchased both house and land, and made them into a small estate. After a hundred years of ownership by the Bedfords, the 80 acres and Pew Hill House was sold in 1793 to John Heath, also of Chippenham, for £3,000. This was the beginning of another use for land at Cocklebury, a use one third of it is put today: to provide living accommodation near enough to Chippenham for the owners to be able to work there, and yet far enough out for them to be away from the dirt, noise and people of a busy town.

At the time of his purchase of Pew Hill House and its land, John Heath practised law in Chippenham. He constantly handled the leasing and selling of land at Cocklebury, as did another attorney of Chippenham, Anthony Guy. There are many links with the Guy family at Cocklebury. Their family history is at first confusing, until it is realised that in every generation there was an attorney called Anthony Guy. Their story begins with a marriage at Chippenham between one Anthony Guy and Ann Hathrel on 6 October 1667. The Guys played an active role in the affairs of Chippenham until the last of the family left in 1830. In 1723, the family is recorded as leasing or occupying land at Cocklebury. Gradually they acquired property south and east of the Pew Hill estate, approximately where the railway cutting is today. By 1820, the last Anthony Guy at Chippenham had purchased Cocklebury farmhouse and land surrounding it. It was undoubtedly he who altered the house by enlarging it turning it from a working dwelling into a more elegant structure, suitable for the home of a well-to-do attorney.

The same Anthony Guy, with his business associate, Edward Michell (later to marry a member of the Edridge-Esmead family, the purchasers of Monkton manor from the Seymours), handled the sale of Rawlings farm at Cocklebury to Robert Ashe of Langley Burrell manor. Their final account to the Reverend Ashe reads: 'To a great many attendances on yourself and Mr. Fast [the previous owner of Rawlings] to negotiate this purchase which after a great deal of trouble was affected'. They charged £220, a considerable sum for a sale of £5,025. Part of the 'great deal of trouble' was the preparation of a list or schedule, as it was called, of all previous owners of the property, with the necessary documents of proof attached. The schedule and all papers concerning the negotiations of this sale are among the papers of the Ashe family at the Wiltshire Record Office.

The list or schedule started in 1664 when William Bayliffe sold 'all the lands . . called and known by the name of Rawlings' to Henry Goldney.It may be recalled, the Goldneys, alias Affarnells, originally purchased the land in the early 1500s. Obviously they had since sold it, perhaps during a time of slump in the cloth trade, when capital was urgently needed. Now the position was reversed. William Bayliffe needed capital, no doubt for the rebuilding of Monkton House. So he sold Rawlings for £1,250, with legal expenses of five pounds and a few shillings, to Henry Goldney.

Henry's eldest son inherited Rawlings, and it became part of a financial setlement made at the time of his marriage to one Elizabeth Speke Pett. It was to be used for her support if she became a widow and after her death to be passed on to their eldest son (the assumption being made that the marriage would be fruitful, which it was). After 19 years of marriage, Elizabeth was brought by her husband before an ecclesiastical court in 1732, to answer to a charge of adultery. Whether the marriage agreement concerning Rawlings was nullified by this action has not been discovered, but by 1740 control of the estate had passed to their son Henry, who installed Edwin and Mary Gale as tenants there.

At the time Henry Goldney was having financial troubles (later he gave up his business as a clothier and moved to Winchester). A few years before, he had mortgaged Rawlings to John Jones, a drugget maker of Derry Hill. By 1752, John was able to foreclose the mortgage and purchase the estate for £1,700. John Jones was related to the Gale family at Cocklebury. They had been living for a very long time on 'ye hill' there (surely the origin of Pew Hill?). The tenancy of Rawlings was granted to one of the Gale sons, and their family continued to occupy the farm for at least two more generations.

In his will Jones left Rawlings in trust for John, the son of Nathaniel Fast, a neighbouring weaver of Derry Hill. Why? Was John Fast a namesake godchild of his, or did he owe Nathaniel money and this was a way of paying off his debt? The answer is not likely ever to be known. Rawlings eventually became John Fast's property and remained so until, evidently having no family to inherit, he sold the house and its farmland to the Ashes in 1820. Rawlings then became a part of Langley Burrell manor estate, and has remained so ever since.

These purchases at Cocklebury by the various families mentioned are comparatively easy to trace amongst the deeds at the County Record Office. Not so easy to find are the transactions of the Esmead-Edridge family of Monkton, for many of their legal records of the estate are apparently lost or were destroyed in the bombing of Bristol during the Second World War. So the main source of information for these records are the Chippenham and Langley Burrell parish tithe books, the Chippenham Town records and the Wiltshire Record Office.

From all of these records the fate of Cocklebury farm can be determined. Towards the end of the century it belonged to, and was occupied by, a William Woody. He sold it to Anthony Guy, who lived there for five years and then sold out to Thomas Edridge of Monkton. The Scott farm at Cocklebury also came into his possession. It had been held by the Scott family for 200 years, but about the time Henry Goldney moved to Winchester because of financial difficulties, the Scotts were also in trouble, and began to sell the farm piece by piece. At first, ownership was divided amongst several persons who rented out its small fields, such as Champions and Nicholasmead, for grazing. After 1820, Thomas Edridge began to buy these parcels of land, and totally owned the farm by 1829.

The common field known as Chippenham, Cocklebury and Langley Burrell field lay between the bottom of Pew Hill and Monkton House. Originally divided into strips and farmed individually to the 1500s, for the next 100 years these strips were apparently leased out from their separate owners and farmed in combined blocks. Then the area began to be enclosed and sold off in small sections, creating a form of land speculation indulged in by yeoman farmers, clothiers and gentlemen alike. John Powell's map of 1784 shows this area south of Cocklebury lane being farmed as arable, and rightly so, for it lay above the Cornbrash, and was the most suitable for such crops. Parts of the fields are given their original names on the map (for example, Little Moor and Gales Moor), but other sections are already enclosed and bear newer names such as Tynings or Greenditch. (The latter was a name in use until the field was swallowed up by the Monkton housing estate.)

The first purchases, in the area between Pew Hill and Chippenham Clift, were made by yeoman farmers from Langley Burrell, the Gales, Neates and Elys among them. The Hulberts from nearby Sheldon also entered the sale ring. Finally, as speculation became more expensive, the Edridges and Essingtons, local clothiers, and Joseph Colbourne of Hardenhuish became involved.

Over the years, the Guy family, grandfather, father, son and grandson–all named Anthony–were either legal representatives or buyers of land. By 1824, except for several small plots bordering the Langley road by Chippenham Clift, all of the once common fields were held by the Ashe family, Anthony Guy or Thomas Edridge. And as we have already seen, Edridge purchased the Guy lands soon after.

At this time, Anthony Guy had been a leading and influential figure in Chippenham for at least 30 years. He was honoured and respected, so much so that in 1826 a testimonial dinner had been held for him and in 1829 he became Mayor of the town. But Anthony Guy's financial affairs were in disarray, and he had been skating on a very thin sheet of honesty for quite some time. In 1830 he was declared bankrupt, at 2s 4½d in the pound. There is much more to relate about Anthony Guy and a rich source of material awaits a biographer of this flamboyant character. Unfortunately, it is beyond the scope of this book to tell his story, but one part pertains to Cocklebury and hence will be considered in some detail. This part also reveals the solution to one of the mysteries of Chippenham history, the disappearance by the 1700s of lands donated to the parish church or its chantries during medieval times.

In 1833 commissioners appointed by Parliament to protect such charities as these lands inquired into the deposition of income accruing from their rents. It was certainly Anthony Guy's bankruptcy that prompted them to investigate the charity at this particular time, for the bankruptcy had ended his 26-year stewardship of the church lands. They soon discovered the total loss of the bulk of the donated church lands, at least 40 parcels. This they could not blame on Anthony Guy, for the disappearance had occurred as far back as his grandfather or great-grandfather's time. But they did find that he had falsified accounts, not recorded rent payments, and sold three-quarters of an acre of church property dishonestly, for he represented it as belonging to him. (He had sold it to a Mr. Bailey, a descendant of the Bayliffe family, who became a bankrupt himself a few years later.)

From the 12th century to the 14th, at least forty small pieces of land or property in and around Chippenham had been donated to the parish church or its chantries. Of these, more than half lay in Cocklebury or in the adjoining common fields of Chippenham and Langley Burrell. By the time Anthony Guy had ended his stewardship, the church lands consisted of ten parcels, one only at Cocklebury. This was a cottage, with orchard, garden and pasture for one cow, probably the one still standing today in Cocklebury lane, just beyond the entrance to Rawlings farm. The rent of this cottage was not being received by the church, however, but by William Woody, at one time owner of Cocklebury farm. He admitted to receiving the rent, but implied that it was being used to support a pauper lunatic!

The church commissioners failed to solve the mystery of the whereabouts of the missing land. They confined themselves to commenting that they 'found it utterly impracticable to trace parcels of property specified' and concluded that they 'had scarcely ever known an instance of such protracted and culpable neglect on the part of a whole body of feoffees [stewards, which of course, included Anthony Guy, and at one time, the attorney, John Heath of Pew Hill House] both in respect to preservation of property, and receipt and application of the funds, which it was their duty to administer'. Scathing criticism indeed!

Where had the lands gone? From existing church records, during the 15th and 16th centuries they were rented to residents of Chippenham, who presumably farmed or sublet them. Many familiar Cocklebury names crop up in these early rent rolls. Payne, Oliver, de Cokelberg, Champion, Sambourne, and Rawlings are early on the list, and by 1490, John Goldney. Baker, Scott, Self, Parry, Bayliffe, Gale, Stafford, Hulbert, and Bull all appear in the 1500s. But in 1559, more than 20 years after the Reformation, lands 'late of St Mary's Chantry'. in Chippenham town and Downham field in Cocklebury were granted by the Crown to John Cuttle and Richard Roberts. Neither were heard of again. A year later, Henry Goldney of Chippenham purchased Crown chantry lands, as did Edward Westfield. In 1581, several tenants of church lands at Cocklebury, listed above, plus Thomas Goldney and other members of the same family granted the use of these lands to William Bayliffe of Monkton. Rents from these lands were then no longer recorded in church records. Nearly a hundred years later, several closes at Cocklebury–Paynes, Champions, Moore meadow and Downham–were mortgaged by William Bayliffe. All had once been listed as church property at Cocklebury; now they were obviously privately owned.

Meanwhile, the enclosure of the remaining common fields of Langley Burrell, Chippenham, and Cocklebury had begun. The process was slow, but in the next 100 years many transactions dealing with small parcels of land took place in this area, including parcels once belonging to Chippenham parish church. As the current Anthony Guy or John Heath handled these transactions, and as parcels of church land in the area were in private hands by the end of the century, the conclusion seems obvious. The church lands were appropriated by private citizens, and then by arrangement taken off the records of the parish church. Later they would be sold privately. Further research would surely prove that this too was the fate of other church property located not only at Cocklebury, but also in and around Chippenham.

By 1829, however, all land dealing at Cocklebury had ceased, and the area was consolidated into three main sections: Pew Hill estate; Rawlings; and the lands owned by Thomas Edridge of Monkton. These included the old Scott farm, leased to a John Vines, and Cocklebury Farm, rented to a Thomas Cole. Common fields (such as Great and Little Moore, the Quarry Ground, Sadler's Mead and others along the river) became parkland around Monkton House, transformed by the planting of hard wood trees and permanent leys. Several houses had been built along Langley road, and Langley Burrell manor owned some fields in the Pew Hill area. For ten more years, until the coming of the railway, land use at Cocklebury was to remain static.

As a result of these land transactions at Cocklebury, several houses emerged that are still in existence today. Although W. G. Hoskins has called the period from about 1570 to 1640 the great age of rebuilding in rural England, at Cocklebury rebuilding extended into the 19th century, a reflection of the continued prosperity and growth of the area. There were several reasons for rebuilding. Monkton and Pew Hill House were altered and extended, to meet the needs of two successful families and their social aspirations. Fashion, however, was a second thought when Cocklebury and Rawlings farmhouses were enlarged to deal with the demands of a new way of farming and the increasing production of cheese during the 18th century.

The consolidation of the farms at Cocklebury made several farmhouses redundant. Unlike the Scott dwelling, these houses have survived, converted to serve non-farming households. Both Avon House at Pew Hill and a house at 11 Langley Road hide within them original farmhouses, of similar design to Cocklebury. A cluster of cottages at the side of the entrance to the driveway to Monkton House was once a farmhouse, which lost its use as such when the railway came through the area, and the land around it was turned into roads. All these vernacular houses are structually the same as they were 150 years ago. There are records showing that many cottages existed at Cocklebury up to the 19th century, but only one still stands. It was constructed of rubble stone while its companions, built of wattle or timber and daub, have totally disappeared. No traces of their foundations can be found; only an occasional well shaft marks their site.

At Cocklebury today by far the most important building architecturally is Monkton House. It will be recalled that the manor was sold by the Seymour family in 1686. The sale probably came as a great shock to William Bayliffe, tenant of the manor at the time, for his father 20 years before the sale had signed a second 99-year lease with the Seymours. Soon after, on the security of this lease, he converted the old timbered manor house into an elegant stone mansion, as depicted in an estate map of 1710. It was very similar in style to Asby House, Ashdown, Berkshire, built about 1665. As there was no parkland at the time, William Bayliffe created a formal garden between the front of the house and the river, consisting of four rectangles of grass bordered by wide paths. This arrangement was enclosed by a high turreted wall to keep out cattle. At the foot of the garden by the river, the mooring place held a small boat, such as that mentioned in Elizabeth Bayliffe's 1705 probate inventory, ready to convey family, guests, or servants to Chippenham on the opposite bank. The house and its pleasure garden fitted snugly into the surrounding landscape, neither one too pretentious for the other.

About a hundred years later, Esmead Edridge, the great-grandson of the purchaser of the manor in 1686, converted William Bayliffe's Jacobean house, quite simply and without great expense, to a fashionable Georgian style house of the time. It was very similar to two other houses in the neighbourhood, 45 St Mary Street (which probably belonged to Monkton estate) and Hardenhuish House, built in 1774 by a business associate of the Edridge family, Joseph Colbourne. Like its predecessor, the surroundings of the new house at Monkton were not pretentious, but the later creation of a park made a tremendous difference to the setting, giving the Edridges the opportunity to proclaim that it ws the home of a family of wealth and local stature. The house depicted in the 1710 estate map had two storeys, with seven bays and attic dormer windows in the front. There were five bays on each side and a square front porch supported by two ionic columns. A pediment at roof level covered three front bays, and a central round cupola fronted by a parapet appeared above the roof.

For his house, 100 years later, Esmead Edridge retained the same number of bays, the porch and the pediment, but the roof was raised to create another storey with bays matching those below. The cupola remained, though changed in shape, and the parapet was moved forward to be in line with the face of the building. Inside, rooms were enlarged, but the original layout of reception rooms in front and kitchen and diverse domestic offices behind did not change. Upstairs, the number of servants' bedrooms were increased. Presumably, following the fashion of the times, the newly-created top floor was intended for nursery rooms. Whether they were to be used as such is another matter, for the house seemed always to be lived in by childless members of the family, and the estate usually passed from cousin to cousin, never from father to son. The suggestion has been made that the famous Bath firm of Wood and Sons were responsible for the design of Hardenhuish House. It is quite possible that Esmead Edridge consulted the firm at the time of his inheritance (1778, four years after Hardenhuish House was built) regarding alterations to both Monkton and 45 St Mary Street, as the architectural features of the three houses are strikingly similar.

A description of the house in 1791 from the Universal British Directory says: 'Mouncton House, the seat of Esmead Edridge, Esq., is only separated from Chippenham by the River Avon, and a gradually-sloping lawn terminated by the building, of which there is a pleasing view from one of the streets near the churchyard'.

The house retains its 18th-century exterior today. Its setting has been altered for houses of the Monkton estate have been built behind it on part of the parkland belonging to the house. But they are not obtrusive, for a gentle slope of land partially hides them, and the remainder of the parkland along the Avon still provides a fine frame for the gracious house. It is fortunate that Chippenham Borough Council, after purchasing Monkton House in 1954, recognised its classic beauty and left it unaltered, for such an example of architectural skill, seldom practised today because of high costs and the lack of masonry skills, deserves to be protected.

Rawlings farmhouse, in common with Monkton House, still retains the same exterior of its final rebuilding. 'A mapp of an Estate called Great Rawlings at Cocklebury near Chippenham belonging to Henry Goldney, Gent', drawn in 1725, depicts the house almost as it is today (it lacks two attic dormers), but it is difficult to pinpoint the actual time of this final rebuilding. A date over the porch reads 1697, but before the 19th century such dates can be misleading, and do not necessarily imply rebuilding at that particular time. Another date on a cornerstone, 1764, and the initials RG and JG (standing for Robert Gale, the tenant at the time, and his brother John) is also deceptive, for that cornerstone was certainly in position when the estate map was drawn forty years previously.

The local stone walls, set with mullioned windows, could have replaced a timbered building at any time in the 17th century. The quality of the masonry is good, and the enlargement of the house, for its time, is on an extensive scale; so it is possible that the rebuilding took place at the instigation of Henry Goldney after he purchased the estate in 1664. Rawlings remains a working farmhouse as it was when originally built. It is of excellent proportions with its high-hipped roof and two rows of mullioned windows in the front. An extension on the east wall does not detract from the proportions of the main building. There have been many alterations to the interior of Rawlings, as recent work on its old kitchen in the middle of the house has revealed. Over the original central hearth site is an enormous fireplace and within are at least three others, each smaller than the previous one. The floor of this room was once a foot lower than it is today, as are the foundations of the back wall of the house. This central room may well have been the extent of the first dwelling on the site, quite possibly as far back as Saxon times. There are two other levels of the ground floor, on either side of the central room, indicating that one room was expanded to two and finally to three.

Upstairs, the same pattern of three rooms occurs, with one of the bedrooms leading into another, probably a parent-child arrangement. This lay-out afforded very little privacy but, except for the rich, this was still not expected at the time. Later the area was partitioned into smaller rooms, and an interior stairway built to the attic. This was doubtless installed after the need for cheese storage in the attic had ceased towards the end of the 19th century and the space could be used for servant accommodation.

The 1725 estate map depicts the farmhouse surrounded by orchards on two sides, with a substantial barn on the west and a small gate placed to allow passage to the front door in the hedge facing the house. There is no indication of any kind of cow sheds or yard behind the house to accommodate cows for milking or to shelter cattle from bad weather. So it can be presumed in 1725 that the cows were milked in the fields and the milk brought back to the cheese room, built onto the back of the house at the same time as the extension on the east wall. The cheese room today has its original flagstone floor, small windows and two doors. One leads into the house, the other is near the outside entrance where cheeses for storage were hauled up by rope and pulley to the attic.

In contrast to Rawlings, the appearance of Cocklebury farmhouse today is quite different from the 18th century, when it was a simple stone house of one room up, one down, and a buttery. Early on in the same century, probably at about the same time the cheese room at Rawlings was built, a cheese room with a loft above was constructed a little distance away from the house, at a right angle to it. This allowed, almost a century later, the two buildings to be linked to form an 'L'-shaped building. The linkage, really an addition, was made by Anthony Guy, and is vaguely Regency style. A staircase was built in this section, for until this time the upper floors could only be reached by ladders. It is well proportioned and the mason went to a great deal of trouble to match cornerstones and to link the two buildings so that the eye is not drawn to the area of the joins. The sash windows in this section indicate a date of construction around 1820. The basic 'L' shape of Cocklebury remains today, hidden somewhat by additions made in past years to accommodate dairy equipment needed to cool and ship liquid milk.

During the 18th century, sheds for 40 or more cows and a stable for six horses were built to the north and east of the farmhouse. These formed a large sheltered area for cattle, and enabled them to be kept closer to the cheese room at milking time. Cheese making produces large quantities of whey. When cooked with potatoes and barley, as was the custom in the 18th century, it is a perfect food for pigs. In the Vale, pigsties were always built near the cheese room to convey the whey to the pigs more easily. Cocklebury farm was no exception, and the pigsties there were connected with underground pipes to transport the whey, a labour-saving device.

John Powell's map of 1784 clearly shows the house and these farm buildings. Their placement cut right across the old track, which ran alongside the farmhouse and continued on to Cocklebury Common and Monkton House. A new track was made to the east, to be bridged over 100 years later when the cutting for the Calne railway line was dug out.

Another farmhouse at Cocklebury probably existed on the present site of Pew Hill House. It is likely that the Norbornes converted it to their needs. Later, the Bedfords and the Heaths expanded the dwelling to provide for their family needs and social status. Pevsner describes the present house as being built in 1895 by Silcock and Reay in local Tudor and Stuart style. This may just apply to the exterior, for an 1840 sale description of the house depicts it as large as it is today, and parts of the interior certainly belong to an earlier period.

The evolution of Avon House in Cocklebury lane by Pew Hill (now, like Pew Hill House, being used as office accommodation for the Westinghouse Brake and Signal Company) began as a farmhouse of similar design to that of Cocklebury. The need for a farmhouse in that particular site ceased probably in the 18th century, when the land was incorporated into the Pew Hill House estate. In 1873, Kilvert, the diarist, mentions a school situated at Avon House, run by a Miss Gale. A large addition to the house was constructed in Victorian times, but whether before or after the school was there is not known. The addition, however, meant that the old farmhouse became another Cocklebury dwelling to be converted to the needs of a non-farming household.

The back of Clift House (as it was called until recently) at 11 Langley Road, was once a small 17th-century farmhouse, again similar to Cocklebury, with a step-down buttery between two rooms serving as kitchen and living room on the ground floor, and one large room above with elm floor boards. Again, the need for a farmhouse there had ceased to exist, so in the early 19th century, by the addition of four rooms and a staircase behind a simple Regency front, the farmhouse was transformed into a town house of good taste and style.

One other vernacular building deserving mention is the cottage by the track between the two railway bridges. Built around 1800, undoubtedly on the site of another dwelling, the cottage has a mansard, tiled roof typical of the Chippenham area of that time, and stone rubble walls. Originally there were flagstones on the ground floor and elm boards in the bedroom. It was the simplest of cottages, one room downstairs with a fireplace, and a sleeping area upstairs under the rafters. Provided with a quarter acre of ground, its tenant was able to grow potatoes and keep a pig. The author remembers the outhouse at the bottom of the garden, the well by the entrance door, and a pig in the sty. Within, multi-coloured rugs made out of scraps of material hooked into sack cloth covered the flagstones; a dark red cloth edged with bobbles hid the white deal top of the kitchen table; and the cooking was done on a small, formidable black grate with an oven by the side. The chimney smoked, and in the winter innumerable draughts came through the poorly-fitting windows and door. It was a tied cottage and although not a comfortable dwelling, it was situated conveniently for the tenant working at Cocklebury farm less than a quarter of a mile away.

Although more speculation in land at Cocklebury took place in the 18th and early 19th centuries than at any other time in its history, the most important use of the area still was to produce food. To farm successfully at Cocklebury at this time a tenant had to have at least 60 acres of productive land, and a willingness to adjust to new methods of production. In no way, however, had the adjustment to be as rapid as it is for the farmer today.

The 1700s saw the tentative beginnings of scientific farming. Rudimentary attempts at selective breeding of cattle began amongst some of the Vale farmers, and the Chippenham area received particular attention from agricultural writers. It was beginning to be understood that a greater variety of fertilizers could improve crop yields and contribute to keeping the land in continual good heart. And on many farms, including those at Cocklebury, some form of primitive drainage was being carried out on the clay soils. There was a much greater emphasis on the production of milk for cheese making and the fattening of beef cattle, since the expanding population of England meant a larger market for veal, beef, bacon and lamb, all of which could be profitably raised on the high-yielding grasslands of the Vale. Inevitably, arable crops acreage declined, and farmers either grew just enough oats, barley and pease needed for their own use, or bought from local markets to fulfil their needs. The beef and dairy cattle were the greatest producers on the farms at Cocklebury. Mature animals to be fattened for beef were obtained from Devon or Hereford. They were then grazed either for six or for 18 months before being ready for market. Today this would be considered a long time to produce a beef animal, but two factors were involved. The market demanded a larger, fattier animal than is desired today, and in the 18th century supplementary feeding was not usually enough to maintain weight during the winter. Consequently the animal lost poundage, and needed time in the spring to replace its original weight and gain once more. It was customary to keep beef cattle out all the year round, and at Cocklebury they were no doubt grazed in the meadows by the river. In winter they would be fed daily with hay, and towards the end of the century oil cake provided additional sustenance.

Calves from both beef and dairy cattle were another source of profit. They were fattened by suckling, then slaughtered at the age of about two months, the carcass being quartered and sent to market by cart. Some calves were raised until they were six months old and presumably would then go to market under their own steam!

Dairy cattle in the Vale were exclusively Longhorns in the 18th century. Originally, farmers purchased them from markets such as Highworth, near Wootten Bassett, where they were sold after being driven down from the Midland counties. Later the farmers themselves began to breed cattle, though still purchasing their bulls from the Midlands to avoid interbreeding. William Marshall, that stalwart of agricultural observers, spent some time in the Chippenham area visiting farms and talking to their owners or tenants. A Mr. Beames at Avon drew the most praise:

> 'He has forty cows, which, in mould–though not size–may vie with any dairy of caws the Midland country can produce; and has this season (1788) a lot of the evenest and the most beautiful yearling heifers I have ever seen in any country . . . it may be said without risque, that, at present, no district in the kingdom, of equal extent, can show such herds of cows.'

High praise indeed, but what superlatives William Marshall would have used had he seen the fine pedigree cattle in the district today.

Sheep were run with cows on dairy farms in the Vale. From probate inventories it is evident Cocklebury farms always had a great number of sheep (William Bayliffe in 1673 ran 122 sheep and lambs for instance), but the proportion of sheep to cattle probably lessened considerably towards the end of the century. Unlike south Wiltshire, in the Vale little attention was paid to their breeding and most were sent to market yearly. Their ability to crop grasses shorter than did cattle was apparently important to the dairy farmer. Marshall says 'sheep are run with the cattle to nibble out the choicest herbage' and so, in the opinion of the time, lowered the richness of the pasture. It was thought that the less luxurious pasture produced a better milk for cheese making. The sheep were also beneficial to the grasslands for their qualities of manure production and scattering, while their smaller hooves do not churn up the ground in the winter as do the heavier, larger cattle hooves (as can be seen by the sea of mud at the gateway of any field in the Vale with grazing cattle in the winter). An 1806 lease of Bullhide farm near Allington, partially on the Kellaways Clay, included a clause that the lessee agreed 'to winter and feed the cattle in the skillings or bartons of the said premises . . . so that the land may have the benefit of being winter-bound and not trod with cattle except sheep'. Perhaps this practice was carried out at Cocklebury on some fields, but most of them, particularly those on the Kellaways Sands, were certainly able to carry cattle all the year round without too much destruction to grass.

Pigs at Cocklebury in the 18th century were probably of the long-eared Wiltshire White variety, sometimes cross-bred. They were fattened to a very high weight before slaughter, around 30 score pounds, whereas the pig today goes to market at a third that weight. As has been mentioned before, pigs were always raised on dairy farms to consume the whey from cheese making. And as a regular producer of income, the pig was known in the 19th century as 'the gentleman who paid the rent'.

Slowly-changing farming practices of the 18th century made the production of cheese at Cocklebury the most financially-rewarding agricultural occupation. Better breeding and selection of dairy cows produced longer lactations to be spaced over the year. Previously, cows in a herd calved in the spring and ended their milk production after about six months, so no winter milk ensued. The improvements in methods of fertilization of pastures and meadows produced more hay, which in turn meant more winter feed for the dairy cattle, giving a continuing milk supply during the colder months. More adequate shelter for the dairy animals, such as the yards and cow sheds around the farmhouses provided, also contributed to not only an increasing milk yield, but made it much easier for the dairymaid to maintain quality cheese production in cooler weather. For with the cheese room right by the yards, there was no opportunity for the milk to cool on its journey from the cow to the cheese room, as it would have done had the cows been milked in the fields.

Cheese making was hard work, and along with the milking went on twice a day, every day of the year. Most of the work seems to have been done by women, although it is likely, except at haymaking and harvesting, that men milked the cows and brought the heavy containers of milk to the cheese room. Here the process of cheese making was carried out by a dairymaid (in 1773 earning £4 to £7 a year, depending on experience), but the final responsibility of creating a fine cheese rested totally on the farmer's wife, who gave every step of the operation her closest supervision.

Immediately after milking, while it was still warm, the milk was brought into the cheese room in wooden tubs. These were large enough to be used to set the milk in. Rennet, an extract of calf's stomach containing a coagulating enzyme, would then be added to the milk with grated annato to give the cheese a deep yellow colour.[1] Depending on the time of year, it took a little over an hour for the curds and whey to form. The curd was then broken up gently by hand into fine particles and the whey ladled off to be conveyed to the pigsties. The curds were hand pressed to release more whey, scalded in hot water to firm them, salted and placed into moulds. After being compressed again by hand, the blocks of curd were wrapped in cloth and compacted in a weighted press. The resulting cheeslings, as they were called, ranging from nine to 12 pounds in weight, were resalted and rewrapped over a period of several days. They were then left to sweat and to grow a coat of blue mould on the outside. The mould died off, or was wiped away, after a few weeks, and the cheeses were transferred to the cheese loft for ripening and storage. (This period in hot summers must have exposed the cheeses to destructive levels of temperature, yet there is no mention at all of this phenomenon in agricultural literature of the times.) Both the lofts at Cocklebury and Rawlings were large enough to store several months' production of cheese, which, from 40 cows, could be as much as eight tons a year.

In order to obtain the best prices, the farmer sold his product to cheese factors at intervals, who conveyed it to Marlborough and other markets, or to Weyhill and Stourbridge Fairs. The final destination of much of the cheese in the Vale, however, was London where it enjoyed a reputation of consistent quality and excellence. Considering the amount of cheese produced in the area in the 1700s, it is odd that Chippenham market did not become reputable as a major trading place for local cheese until the mid-1850s. But until the coming of the railway, it was easier for the factor to transport the cheese by wagon, and later by water, to more distant markets than to accumulate large amounts in Chippenham, as was the practice after 1850.

North Wilts cheese, as the Vale cheese was named, came in specific sizes and a particular shape, later known as a truckle. 'It has a richness, and at the same time, a mildness, which recommends it to many', commented William Marshall on its flavour. Compared to cheeses from other areas, it was much freer of faults, such as poor flavour, heaving or blowing, splitting, pasty consistency, and so on. All such phenomena have now been eliminated by the understanding of their causes, but in the 1700s nothing was known of the microbial and chemical processes involved in the production of cheese. The dairymaid and farmer's wife in the Chippenham area had unwittingly over the years evolved an almost fool-proof system of making good cheese, providing cleanliness was maintained at every stage. The setting of the milk directly after it came from the cow (instead of holding it from evening until morning as was done in other localities) and the short processing time from milking to final pressing, ensured the least amount of contamination from undesirable micro-organisms that could later produce such faults as off-flavours and heaving. North Wilts cheese in all probability resembed a mild cheddar of today, though its short scalding process would have produced a softer textured cheese, unless it was ripened for a considerable length of time such as six months or over.

Besides the production of meat and cheese at Cocklebury, arable crops were still grown on the Cornbrash, as John Powell's map of 1784 shows. Other fields above the Kellaway Sands and Clay are recorded in the 18th century tithe lists as being pasture or meadow lands. On the arable the crops were rotated; wheat every three years, followed by either beans, peas or a grass crop, and then barley. Tenant leases specified that no white straw (wheat, oat, or barley straw) was to be grown in succession, to prevent the soil from being denuded of its nutrients. Apparently turnips were introduced to the Vale for cattle food at the end of the century. It was many years, however, before they were popular enough in north-west Wiltshire to give rise to the subject of what is now considered Wiltshire's own song. Popularly known by a line of its chorus, 'The Vly be on the Turmuts', the song refers to the destructive black-fly which attacks the plant if it is not kept well hoed, along with the pleasures of 'turmet-hoeing'.

The predominance of pasture to arable land and the subsequent rise in the number of stock carried at Cocklebury and other farms in the Vale still did not mitigate the age-old problem of finding enough manure to produce maximum crops of grass and hay. In 1704, tenants of Langley Burrell manor court protested 'that no person ought to take up and carry awy any dung horse or cows . . . or digg and carry away any sand or earth without the consent of the Lord out of Langley Heath or Burch Marsh'. One hundred years later leases of farms specified that all manure and compost be 'laid or spread abraod upon the arable and pasture ground'. In the last year of the lease the manure was to be accumulated, for the next tenant to use as he saw fit. But animal manure was not now enough. A certain amount of liming was practised in the Vale, and it is on record that around Chippenham woollen waste, 'town' manure, wood ashes and rags (no synthetic fibres then) were all used as supplements. Guana and artificial phosphates were not available until the 19th century.

Timber was an important crop in the 18th and 19th centuries, and carefully preserved. In the 1780s Lord Shelburne planted 150,000 trees a year on the Bowood estate near Calne, and all farms in the Vale grew trees for timber. It was the landlord, however, and not the tenant who chiefly benefited from the crop, and age-old rules existed regarding the deposition of all timber and wood on a farm. All hedgerows planted at the time of enclosure, and of course the older hedges, contained several species of trees and tree-like shrubs among their hawthorns and blackthorn. A tenant was expected to nurture the hardwood trees in the hedgerows by leaving them at trimming times in order to grow to maturity. The landlord then decided when they were to be cut and the proceeds of their sale went to him. The oak, elm and ash were the most valued for they were the producers of hardwood.

At Cocklebury, in Tanker ground, an 18th-century deed mentions four elms as part of the field's value. When Rawlings was sold in 1820, an inventory was made of the trees there. In a total of 80 acres, consisting of nine hedged fields and a quarter of a mile of river bank, there were 202 elms, 63 oaks, 60 ashes, 1,544 pollards (small trees suitable for posts), 233 saplings, 198 willows and poplars, three walnut trees and two aspens. Their total value as timber was £605, more than one-tenth the purchase price of the farm itself.

It is not surprising that walnut trees are mentioned, for besides their timber, they were of value for their fruit which was pickled before maturing, or eaten raw when fully ripe. There were walnut trees at Cocklebury known to the author. Two near Monkton House supplied nuts for the residents of Cocklebury farm each Christmas. Another in the garden at 11 Langley Road was more than 100 years old in the 1930s, and most likely was once part of the the hedgerow of the field known as Cocklebury furlong.

Some trees were allowed to grow in the fields to provide shelter for cattle and were also part of the timber crop. The author recalls several such trees at Cocklebury and learned that there were many more at the beginning of this century. These trees made the scene far more attractive than do the empty fields of today. The economics of modern farming do not allow their presence any more, for large trees inhibit the growth of grass around them, and interfere with the movement of machinery in the fields.

Besides the hardwood trees, hedgerows at Cocklebury contained such species as hazel and alder. Holly grew there too. Cracked willow still grows in the older hedges at Cocklebury, and was at one time employed for basket making. Hurdles were constructed from other species of willow planted specially for the purpose, referred to as withy setts. Today the ravages of Dutch Elm disease and farming procedures have drastically reduced the number of trees in the remaining fields of Cocklebury. The number and variety of trees there in the 18th and 19th centuries was greater than at any other time since the Saxon clearances, and is never likely to be matched again.

A tenant was not allowed to claim possession of the large timber trees on his farm when they were felled. He was allowed enough wood from his land for repairs to his house and buildings, to make or repair gates, stiles, fence rails and farm machinery. Dead and hollow trees, the lops, tops, and small branches and other burnable wood from live trees when felled, the brush and faggots resulting from periodic hedge trimming and laying; all these were the farmer's perquisite. Wood from these sources was the only fuel at Cocklebury, the lack of copses making wood needed for cooking and heating a commodity to be used carefully. Those who could not afford to buy wood or coal had to depend on the permission of the farmer to take dead wood from the hedges around the area. There is no mention in any documents or books of the time when the poor obtained their fuel. The growing population and lessening woodlands must have created serious difficulties, until coal could be cheaply transported by canal instead of by cart from Somerset. The poorer inhabitants of Cocklebury probably had to resort to a long walk to Pewsham or Bird's Marsh to supply their needs.

A drainage system today is taken for granted as part of farming on the Clays. Until the 18th century few attempts were made at draining the Vale farms, probably because the problem was so great, although on the nearby and less troublesome chalk, drains from Roman times were still being utilized. The 18th century saw a greater realisation by the working farmer of the need to drain the heavy clay soils and low lying areas of the Vale to increase grass production. An undrained field, especially in the springtime, is colder than a drained field, and the constant wetness interferes with or blocks the aeration of the soil. The new growth of grass is delayed, and continuing wetness produces a rank crop.

Experiments with underground drains, such as channels filled with wood brush, ashes, or stones were not very successful, the chief fault being that the trenches were laid too near the surface. It is evident that little was understood in the Vale of drainage techniques in such soils. Not until the 1840s, with the mass production of clay pipe sections and the availability of cheap–often gang–labour, was tile draining financially possible on a large scale. Then tiles were laid two and five feet under the ground in rows 20 to 50 feet apart. An acre of field with stiff clay soil would need 1,000-2,500 tiles (the number used depending on the distance between the rows) and they cost about £4 to lay. Usually this cost would be divided between the landlord and tenant. Many of the fields at Cocklebury had such drainage systems installed in the mid-1800s, five feet under the surface. Their underground patterns are still visible in aerial photographs today.

With the exception of the stream on its northern boundary, Cocklebury has no other drainage on the surface, only the springs on the dividing line between the Kellaways Clay and Sands. There is no way of knowing how wet its fields once were but with only rudimentary drainage until the mid-19th century, many of its fields on the clay were no doubt constantly saturated, especially in the winter. Residents at the end of Eastern Avenue at the Monkton estate today can dig up from their gardens the ashes put down yearly in the author's time at a gateway once situated on the spring-line between Brake field and Cocklebury Common. In January and February, despite the ashes, that narrow low area became a sea of mud, sometimes a foot deep, due to the passage of the cows being moved twice daily for milking at Cocklebury farm. Apparently this area was never drained, and illustrates how wet certain fields could be in the winter before tile drainage.

Two examples of pre-tile drainage at Cocklebury are definitely known. First, in the Barn ground by Rawlings Farmhouse, wide ridges were made to form shallow ditches across the field from east to west. (William Marshall reports a similar instance of sub-draining at Avon in 1778.) Second, Mr. E. A. Self, who farmed at Cocklebury from 1928 to 1963, has told the author of the existence of a very old drainage channel underneath the fields along the Avon. It emerged at the western end of Monkton Park, opposite the weir on the river. The creation of hedges and ditches at the time of enclosure of the fields at Cocklebury would also have provided some drainage for the area. These ditches were then incorporated into the tile systems of the 19th century. They are still serving the same purpose, for it is still necessary at Rawlings farm to keep certain ditches clear, to ensure the maximum efficiency of the tile drains under the fields.

A manor court at Monkton certainly existed from the time its lands were acquired by Monkton Farleigh Priory in 1150. Under the jurisdiction of the Prior, the court would have maintained the rules of husbandry for the common fields, defined tenant duties, and generally continued the contemporary feudal customs of the area. Slowly these were abandoned, so the need for a court lessened, but the tradition of holding a manor court continued through the centuries until the last one in 1896. The existing records of the court begin in 1733, but their form then indicates that they were a continuation of previously-held courts. Probably that form dates from 1536 when Edward Seymour acquired the lands of Monkton and they were reorganized by his steward, Berwick, into the manor. The commencement date of these records is probably the year that the Esmead family first resided at Monkton.

It will be recalled that the manor was sold in 1686, but the Bayliffes, who held the tenancy until 1765 or for three lives, continued to live at the house. In 1734, a year after the existing court records began, Mary, recent widow of Charles Bayliffe, was awarded by the manor court a tenancy to certain land in the manor granted to her husband in 1686. This 'special admittancy', as it was called (the only one in court records), may indicate that after Elizabeth died in 1705, Mary and Charles became the third Bayliffe generation to lease Monkton, and remained until Charles' death in 1733. The Esmeads then moved into the house. Evidently relations between the two families were amicable for another Bayliffe (George Searle Bayliffe) held the office of steward to the manor court for almost 40 years.

Arthur Esmead, son of the Calne clothier who acquired Monkton, became manorial lord upon the death of his father in 1705. He did not function as such, for he was a lunatic, and his affairs were administered by his family. His sister, Johanna Edridge, was the lady of the manor when the court records begin. Arthur had a long life and it was not until 1778 that his nephew, Johanna's son, Esmead Edridge, inherited from him. Until the cessation of the courts in 1896, it was always a member of the Edridge family who was lord or lady of the manor.

The courts were held at Monkton House, and probably in the parlour room, which in 1673 contained three 'tableboards' and 18 leather chairs, these being suitable accommodation for the officers and jurors of the court. The tenants of the manor were probably seated in less formal chairs 'with rush and spool bottom'. The officers consisted of a steward, constable, tythingman, hayward, breadweigher and 'taster of same', but except for the first two, their duties in 1733 were nominal and their appearance in court a formality.[2]

At first, the most vexatious question for the court was the disposal of offensive waste and the scouring of water courses and ditches. These were supposed to be the duties of the householders (and tenants of the manor) living nearby, but though year after year fines were levied on the same people, the offences continued. Fines were imposed for 'not cleaning the watercourse leading down the Butts to the Star and Garter'; on a butcher, William Bradbury, 'for throwing out of his slaughter house the entrails of his beasts or their blood in the Cook Street'; on Richard and Jane Smith, for erecting a 'House of Office' against Brook lane by the Common Slip and discharging its soil into the lane. Even the Vicar of Chippenham, Rogers Holland, was fined 5s for a similar offence. He never mended his ways or paid his fines, however, for the same case was presented to the court by the constable for many years. As the 18th century progressed, these 'nuisances' occur less frequently in court records. It is likely that at about this time drainage pipes leading to the nearby river were installed under some streets in Chippenham. According to the parish registers the infant mortality rate in the town also began to drop at this time, a sure sign of better hygiene.

The court began to concern itself with the state of the roads in the area, and the repairs needed to the stocks in St Mary Street. The requests to the town's surveyors of highways to mend the roads appeared almost yearly, but after 70 years of complaining, the court gave up on the stocks. The last entry in 1810 concerning their condition notes, 'the stocks are in a ruinous and decayed state and out of repair'. From this comment, it is probably safe to say that the use of this barbaric form of punishment had ceased in Chippenham well before the 19th century.

In 1825, Thomas Edridge, then lord of the manor, notified the court that he had granted Henry Russ of Derriards, yeoman, permission 'to kill any hare pheasant or partridge and seize all such gunes, barriers and greyhounds setting dogs, lurchers and other dogs, ferrets Trammells, Hayes and other Netts snares or engines for taking, killing or destroying of Hares Pheasants and Partridges'. The appointment of a gamekeeper at Monkton at this particular time precedes the Game Act of 1831, which included the right of manor lords to make such an appoinment. Had Thomas Edridge already heard rumours that such a measure was to be allowed?[3] If so, he perhaps felt such a record at the court gave him in advance additional rights of restraint over poachers which he was otherwise to lose. For after the Game Act was passed, the only means of combating poachers was by invoking the civil law of trespass. Previously no one had been allowed to hunt game except those 'qualified by estate or social standing', which of course excluded most of the population of the countryside.

The question of poaching and hunting game at Cocklebury in 1825 is an interesting one. The area was near the town and at the same time poor people were hungry, so poaching must have become a great temptation and perhaps a nuisance to the manor. Whom did Thomas Edridge permit to kill game there? Just the family and their guests, or were tenants, despite their leases, also allowed to shoot? Why were rabbits not included amongst the other game mentioned? For doubtless they were the most numerous of all game at Cocklebury. And was Henry Russ, with these powers granted to him, able to keep poachers away from Cocklebury effectively? Unfortunately, it is unlikely that the answers to these questions will ever be known.

Edward Michell, the Chippenham attorney who handled the sale of Rawlings with Anthony Guy, was appointed steward of Monkton manor in 1817. His stewardship continued after Thomas Edridge's death, and in 1833 he married Anne, Thomas' widow and lady of the manor. Unfortunately, the marriage between what must hve been two friends of long standing only lasted a short while, for he died in 1835.

Soon after the death of her second husband, following the yearly court proceedings, Ann began to provide 'dinner, dessert and wine' for the court officials and jurors. Their 'fervent thanks' are recorded, the thoughtful gesture evidently being greatly appreciated.

Although the court continued until 1896, its annual occurrence gradually became practically a formality. Only one or two matters would be brought to its attention, usually to do with estate management, such as an order for planting willows along the Avon at Monkton. The dinner, dessert and wine continued to be served, however, turning the sitting into something more than a ceremonial occasion.

During the 1870s the Edridge family rented Monkton House to West Awdry, a prominent solicitor in the area. He became Steward of the court, fulfilling the office for almost twenty years. At his death in 1893, he was replaced by a member of the same family, Peter who held the office until the court ceased to be held. It is due to the Awdry family that all the documents relating to the court were preserved and are now part of the Chippenham Town Records.

In its last century, the court lacked authority, accomplished little and seldom collected any fines. But a tradition was being maintained, even if helped along by the annual dinner! But, when any connection with the past had ceased to exist, and no practical function was being fulfilled, the custom of holding a manor court at Monkton had to cease.

Throughout the period of this chapter, routes around Cocklebury altered very little. The important roads to Melksham, Bristol, Malmesbury and Wootton Bassett remained unchanged, but after a Turnpike Trust had been set up for the Great West Road, a new routing of the London to Bath road came through Chippenham. Supposedly, until the town bridge at Chippenham was widened in 1757, it was impossible for wheeled traffic to cross the river via the bridge because it was too dilapidated. It has been said that for a century or more traffic had to cross the river at Cocklebury or farther up stream, and rejoin the road at Monkton Hill or near Stanley, depending on the direction it was going. But there is little evidence from old maps or recent aerial surveys of such a diversion. The likelihood is that the town bridge was able to carry a certain amount of wheeled traffic despite its dilapidated state for so many years, and the ford in the river by Matford field was used only in an emergency.

The track from Pew Hill to Monkton through Cocklebury, a private road, was slightly altered when farm buildings were added to Cocklebury farm. The decision to place these buildings across the track may have been decided by the need to provide an alternative route there, for just above the farmhouse are several springs. Many centuries of use, combined with continual wetness, had deepened the track to impractical levels so the section was, to use modern terminology, by-passed. It remained undisturbed until quite recently, but is now being filled in with rubble and other building wastes.

Dr. Arnold Platts, in his book *The History of Chippenham*, mentions a Thomas Hewlett, who lived in the toll house at Chippenham Clift by Cocklebury lane. He was a gardener at Monkton, and his son, James, became a painter of some renown. Is this the same Thomas Hewlett who occupied Small-Pox House adjoining Champions field when it was offered for sale in 1797?

Although the plague was no longer a threat, smallpox was still a dreaded disease in the 18th century amongst the poor of the countryside and the towns of England. Any measures of assistance, medical attention and, later on, inoculations for the poor, had to be obtained from the parish poor law officers. There were five epidemics around Chippenham in the first half of the century, but no record exists of deaths from smallpox among the people of Cocklebury. It may well be that as cowpox was endemic in cattle at the time, anyone who was in contact with them would gain immunity, and avoid infection with smallpox. Cases of smallpox were often taken to an isolated house or cottage to be nursed and to avoid the spread of the disease. Small-Pox House at Cocklebury may well have been such a house at one time, or have gained its name for being a former isolation site. As the name was in use in 1797 when the house was for sale, it evidently held no connotations of fear for people then.

It is frequently rash to consider court records as reflecting the character of the people of an area. Yet the very lack of offenders from Cocklebury before the Wiltshire Quarter Session in the 18th century may point to it as being an unusually law-abiding community, or one perhaps too busy with their everyday tasks to get into much mischief. Apparently no murders, sheep stealing (a capital offence if committed in the Devizes area), or robberies were committed by its inhabitants. All that can be produced in the way of serious crime is the case of Edward Bryant. He lived at Cocklebury and his sister worked for a farmer at Allington. The farmer refused to pay her wages, so Edward Bryant walked to Allington to see what it was all about. On arrival there he was assaulted by the farmer's servant, but was himself accused of assault! The case came before Grand Jurors, including the current Anthony Guy, in 1735, and was apparently dismissed, for no more was heard of it.

In 1700, Cocklebury was made up of several small dairy farms, an area of common field, Monkton manor land and the Bayliffe farms, Henry Goldney's 80 acres of Rawlings and the small Pew Hill estate. By 1830 the common field area had disappeared and become farmland and parkland. The Pew Hll estate continued as such. Almost all other land at Cocklebury, owned either by Monkton or Langley Burrell manors, formed three dairy farms, Cocklebury, Scotts and Rawlings.

The buildings of the railway at Cocklebury 10 years later was to forge a close link with the outside world, but as will be seen, it did little to change the basic structure of life at Cocklebury.

WILTS, 1797.

For Sale by Auction,

(If not before disposed of by private Contract)

At the KING's-HEAD INN, CHIPPENHAM,

On SATURDAY, the 9th Day of DECEMBER,

At Three o'Clock in the Afternoon,

SEVERAL CLOSES OF EXCEEDING GOOD

PASTURE LAND,

Lying at COCKLEBURY, *near* CHIPPENHAM *aforesaid, let to Tenants at Will,* viz.

A CLOSE, East side of the Small-pox House, containing 2 Acres and three Quarters, more or less, now in the Tenure of W. GOULD.

A CLOSE, West of the said House, containing three Quarters of an Acre, Tenant W. GOULD.

N. B. *The Tenant has Notice to quit the 21st of December.*

A CLOSE, called CHAMPIONS, (with the Tythes thereof) containing by measure 7 Acres, 1 Rood, 20 Perches, in the Occupation of T. HEWLETT.

The said HOUSE, called the SMALL-POX HOUSE, GARDEN, and ORCHARD adjoining, containing by measure 3 Roods, 33 Perches; and Cow LEAZE in Cocklebury Street, occupied by the said T. HEWLETT.

NICHOLAS MEAD, and the Tythes thereof, containing 2 Acres, 3 Roods, 10 Perches, now occupied by W. BOWSHER.

Conditions will be produced at the Time of Sale, by Mr. HEATH, *Attorney-at-Law,* Chippenham.

COOMBS, PRINTER, CHIPPENHAM.

Chapter Eight

The Industrial World Comes to Cocklebury

The arrival of the railway was, for Cocklebury, without question the most important occurrence of the 19th century, yet the forces of change brought with it were very slow to affect much of the area. The subsequent engineering works and other buildings to be located at Cocklebury after the line had gone through were all to be confined to its immediate locale; consequently Monkton House, its parkland and surrounding farms remained untouched by the invasion, and the people of Cocklebury preserved their rural life style well into the 20th century.

As early as 1834, a preliminary plan to build a railway to link London to Bristol had been incorporated into a bill passed in Parliament. At first it was proposed that the line should run south of the Marlborough Downs through Pewsey and Devizes, but later a more northerly way to Bath and Bristol was decided on; hence the line ran by Chippenham. The way was surveyed; the maps were submitted to Parliament and approved in 1839. When the line was marked out, some slight changes were made, but at Cocklebury the original plan prevailed. The line was to separate several fields on the west side from their farms, but two bridges and a crossing were later provided for access. The major land owners involved at Chippenham included the Borough itself, Joseph Neeld of Grittleton, the Edridges and the Ashe family. No speculation in the land along the route the line was to run took place. The prices paid by the newly-formed Great Western Railway Company for this land, when compared with the current values of real estate in the area, were very fair.

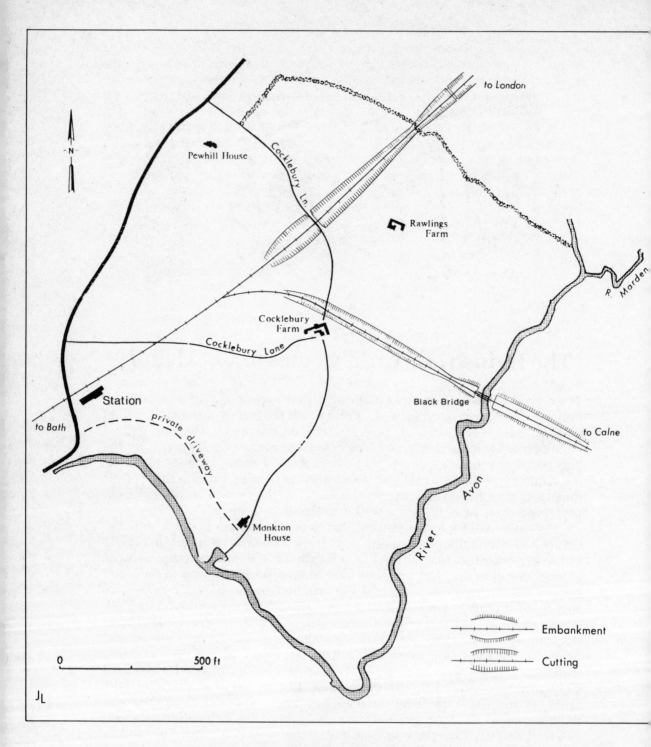

to London

Pewhill House

Cocklebury Ln

Rawlings Farm

R. Marden

Cocklebury Farm

Cocklebury Lane

Station

to Bath

private driveway

Black Bridge

to Calne

Monkton House

River Avon

Embankment

Cutting

0   500 ft

JL

The Railway Network

If the local newspaper of the time, the *Devizes and Wiltshire Gazette*, is any indication, no one realised the effect the railway was to have on their lives. No editorial speculation on the subject was written, and while the line was being built the main journalistic interest concentrated on its progress and the behaviour of the navvies who worked on it.

The section of the line from Wootton Bassett to Bath (which included Cocklebury) proved to be one the most difficult and demanding of all the many feats of engineering needed along the whole line. Isambard Kingdom Brunel, who was appointed at the start of the project as its engineer, had gained worldwide recognition and fame for these feats by the time he had finished seven years later. Like many geniuses, Brunel insisted on having control of nearly everything connected with the enterprise. He had decided its final route and supervised the original survey. He frequently dominated the Company's Board of Directors on financial decisions. He controlled the letting of contracts and often participated in their negotiations, as, for instance, when he arranged a contract for building brick to be obtained from clay pits located at Chippenham (there is no record that the line did receive these bricks, so the contract may have fallen through). He managed the buying of raw materials for the line–the rails, the wooden ties, and even such small items as nails. In the initial stages of construction Brunel lived at the head of the line at Paddington and was on call at all hours. As the line proceeded west beyond London, he spent much of his time in a small hand-driven railway flat which was propelled up and down the line. This took him to where there was trouble, or where his opinion on some issue was needed.

His enormous capacity for detail shows in his influence on the architectural designs and building materials of the bridges, viaducts, the embankments and cuttings all along the line. The viaduct at Chippenham just beyond Cocklebury is a masterpiece of design and strength, and except for some surface deterioration of its Bath stone due to chemical attack from air pollutants today, its condition is as good as when it was built 140 years ago. Perhaps his greatest achievement on the line was Box Tunnel, a few miles down the line from Cocklebury. Built from both ends, the two sections–in all nearly two miles in length–joined up accurately to three-quarters of an inch. Chippenham station was also designed by Brunel, as was the little house opposite where he worked when the line was under construction there. Both were located at Cocklebury, where the cutting becomes an embankment and the Cornbrash and Forest Marble strata emerge from beneath the Kellaways Clay.

The railway engines available to Brunel when the line was planned could not cope easily with a gradient of less than 1 in 100, mainly because of wheel slippage.[1] Hence from Wootton Bassett to Box Tunnel, a series of cuttings and embankments were needed almost continuously to maintain such a gradient, for to follow the local topography would have produced slopes impossible for the engines to haul on. At the time of surveying

engineers would calculate the amount of material needed for an embankment, and whether a nearby cutting could supply. Then the soils and
underlying materials from the cutting, as they were excavated, would be
transported by small tip trucks on a temporary tramway to the nearest
embankment site. The cutting at Cocklebury, a mile long and 50 feet deep,
probably supplied the soils and clay for the embankment which, commenc-
ing at Chippenham station, took the viaduct over to Lowden. For some
reason, perhaps because there was more fill than needed, a huge heap of
Kellaways Clay was left alongside the railway north-east of Cocklebury
bridge. It is still there today, the clay now weathered and covered with
trees, brambles and other undergrowth.

Making the cutting at Cocklebury was heavy work. The surveyed path
of the line to run through the centre of the cutting was marked out by peg
and cord, as were the edges of the cutting. The surface soils were carted
away and the clay excavated to the level that the line was to run, creating a
deep narrow gully. In this gully tram rails were laid on which small tip
trucks were to run. These trucks, pulled by horses, were used to cart the
dirt away from the cutting. Although some blasting by gunpowder was
utilized, the major portion of the excavating was done by pick and shovel,
wielded by imported navvies employed in gangs. As the U-shaped cutting
widened, the danger of slippage of the clay became very great, particularly
in wet weather. Many accidents were caused by slippage, and construction
of the line was delayed for this reason. In fact, slippage is still a problem at
Cocklebury, despite the ballast work carried out at frequent intervals
during the past 140 years.

The *Gazette* devoted much space to slippage accidents, besides
reporting the general progress of the building of the line. The paper dwelt
particularly on the impact of the navvies on the area. They were usually
from the North of England or Ireland, and were hard workers, who spent a
long day with pick and shovel. Their housing consisted of temporary huts,
or tents placed near the site of their work; at Cocklebury, no doubt,
somewhere in the vicinity of the station site, or alongside the cutting. In
1841, one of the construction years, the census records 315 labourers at
Chippenham and nearly 4,000 in all working on the line between Box and
Swindon. So many strangers were bound to have an impact on the area.

The navvies had a reputation for heavy drinking, but they could hardly
be blamed for it; there was little else to do after their working day. Few had
their wives or families with them, and their labour gave them a great thirst.
To the local population they were strangers and communication with them
was difficult; their accents were quite foreign to a Wiltshire 'Moonraker'.
But some communication–or perhaps the more correct word is fraternisa-
tion–did take place, for there was a slight increase in the number of
illegitimate children christened in the parishes of Chippenham and Langley
Burrell for the years the navvies were there.

Accidents were frequent. A few days before the Wootton Bassett-Chippenham section was opened, a tram wagon loaded with sleepers was being pulled by a horse at Cocklebury. An impediment on the rail upset the fast-moving wagon and the sleepers were thrown out onto several labourers. One, seemingly seriously injured, was taken to the *Black Horse Inn* nearby. Luckily he was found to be only severely bruised and returned to work. Another labourer fell across the line while unfastening a horse from a wagon, and a second wagon went over him. He was taken to Chippenham workhouse and it was 'feared an amputation must be performed' as the *Gazette* dolefully stated. Navvies were often injured after incorrectly setting off powder charges for blasting. A freak accident occurred five miles up the line from Cocklebury when a labourer burnt himself to death after falling asleep in a drunken stupor next to a burning lime kiln.

At last the day came when the line was completed between Wootton Bassett and Chippenham. Large sums of money had been offered to the various gangers to induce their men to finish on time. The *Gazette* stated that the men worked 'by night as well as by day, not even allowing the Sunday as a day of rest. In short, by taxing human strength to its very utmost they were enabled to lay down one line of rails just before the arrival of the experimental train on Sunday–the last screw being driven in a few minutes before the train made its appearance'.

The first train down the line the next day (31 May 1841) carried various local officials, and 'Mr. Brunel was with the engine'. A public breakfast held afterwards at Chippenham was attended by the mayor and important citizens of the town. There is no further mention of Brunel; he presumably continued down the line with the engine to Box Tunnel, where there was still trouble. The day was regarded as a local holiday, and Cocklebury residents stood along the top of the cutting to see the first train down the line. Among them was a young girl, later married to a railway worker, who, 70 years later, recalled that this first train was decorated with evergreens. Kilvert, the diarist, recorded in 1875 the recollections of a man who was working by the line that day. 'It was a hot day . . . and I heard a roaring in the air. I looked up and thought that there was a storm coming down from Christian Malford roaring in the tops of the trees, only the day was so fine and hot. Well the roaring came nigher and nigher, then the train shot along and the dust did flee up.'

There was one other delay to the opening of the line between London and Bristol–flooding in the Box Tunnel–which was not rectified until the following month. Then, with very little ceremony, the first train completed the 118-mile journey on 30 June 1841. It took four hours, a very long time for the passengers in open carriages; but within a few years, with more powerful engines, the journey had been cut to two hours. For the first time in its history the people of Cocklebury, if they had the fare, the time and the desire, could travel faster than the speed of a horse.

Except for the Edridges and the residents of Pew Hill House, it is unlikely that they did so, for farmers were notorious for travelling no further than their local markets (and considering the ties of a farm, how could they?), and it was to be many years before a labourer could afford a train journey. At first the fare from Chippenham to Bath was 1s, a tenth of his weekly wage. Later fares were reduced, and there were many offerings of special excursion fares–to the Crystal Palace Exhibition in 1851, for instance. But it was probably not until 1870 or so, when the purchasing power of the agricultural labourer had begun to rise, that a farm worker from Cocklebury could afford to travel on a train.

The presence of the railway soon made changes in the everyday routine at Cocklebury, but once these had been adjusted to, life went on much the same. For a few years after the line was built, there were no bridges across it at Cocklebury, so fields west of the line were severed from their farms and the cattle had to be driven over the tracks to reach their grazing areas. The GWR eventually bought land from the Ashe family for £350 at two locations at Cocklebury and built a bridge at each, so connecting the fields to their farms again. Just above Chippenham station the line cut across Cocklebury lane. A crossing was created there and the GWR made an agreement with Ann Michell of Monkton House to keep the road and the right of way there. It was to be not less than 18 feet in width. This would allow 'visitors, tradesmen, workmen, Servants and agents . . . at all times . . . by night and by day . . . to pass and repass with or without Horses, Cattle and other Animals Carts Waggons and other Carriages respectively laden or unladen' to reach Cocklebury farm. By 1853 the first engineering works at Cocklebury had been built near the crossing, and so it had to be closed. No more could cows from Cocklebury farm graze in the fields of Cowleaze and Cocklebury furlong. A few years later construction of other buildings began there; the use of these fields had changed for good from rural to urban.

The line from Chippenham to Calne, built through Cocklebury in 1861, is likely to have had more impact on the lives of the people living there than did the GWR main line from London to Bristol. Calne line trains were more visible to people at Cocklebury, for unlike the main line trains they ran mostly on a level with the fields or on top of the embankment before the Black Bridge. The main line trains with their larger carriages were longer and faster, and hence somehow more impersonal. In contrast, the little steam railway cars and engines pulling small freight wagons to Calne and back came through the fields every hour or so. Workers on the farm got to know the engine drivers, and the times the trains were expected. This provided a way of telling the time, for few (if any) agricultural workers could afford a watch until well into the 20th century. When the author worked at Cocklebury, a tardy train invariably evoked the comment: 'train be late today', and an early one might stop before going into the station, giving an opportunity for a few words to be shouted back and forth.

The seven-mile line was first proposed in 1859 for a reason probably unique in railway history. The Harris family of Calne had had a continually-growing bacon curing business since the previous century. Irish pigs were the main source of their raw material, so to speak, for Calne was on the Bristol to London drovers' routes. With the introduction of ice into the bacon curing process, allowing it to continue all the year round, their volume of business expanded and quickly exceeded the capacities of local transportation to take their products to Chippenham station for distribution to other parts of the country. So the Harrises proposed the building of a branch line from Chippenham to Calne to bring pigs to their factory and to take the finished pork products out. £35,000 capital was privately raised, of which the family subscribed over half.

The line opened in 1863 with very little ceremony: freight trains began to run immediately, passenger trains a few days later. The *Gazette* commented 'starting from the Great Western line at Chippenham between the Station and engine house, it curves round to the back of Cocklebury farmhouse, from whence it runs in a perfectly straight direction to Stanley Abbey'. A short cutting and embankment were built at Cocklebury, this time through some of its oldest fields–Mancroft, Nicholasmead and Champions–and the apple orchards of Cocklebury farm. Just east of the farmhouse, the cutting severed the lane. An attractive little arched stone bridge, still intact today, was built to span the cutting and to link the lane again.

Neither embankments or cuttings presented serious engineering difficulties, but the bridge over the river turned out to be more complicated. It consisted of eight wooden spans supported on stone abutments. A year before the line opened engineers advised that the wooden girders and flooring needed strengthening; obviously there was no Mr. Brunel to check the design before it was built. After many years the bridge was replaced by a steel structure, painted in dark colours and thus earning the name 'Black Bridge'. It was disassembled in great haste after the line closed in 1963. Today only the stone abutments survive as a reminder of the bridge's existence for 100 years. Local gossip suggested the haste in taking the bridge down was to make sure that the line could never be reopened, but it is more likely that the bridge was considered an attraction for vandals and could provide the scene of an accident if someone fell from it. No doubt the author risked her life many times when she and childhood friends regularly clambered about the structure, feeling very wayward and daring. The path of the line today is now a nature walk, and at the time of writing is serving as a barrier to further urban growth on Cocklebury land.

Until 1850, Chippenham's only manufacturing enterprises were the making of woollen cloth and silk. Evidently, during the Industrial Revolution the town was not considered a suitable site for the location of new manufactories, probably because of the distance from coal sources, and the lack of direct transportation by canal. Ralph Gaby, a Chippenham

personage involved in several business enterprises, acquired in 1812 a
financial interest in the creation of a tramway to link the Forest of Dean
coalfields via a canal to Chippenham. Whether the venture was successful
has not been discovered, but coal began to come into the area in quantity
after the opening of the Wilts and Berks canal in 1810. The price soon
became much lower. At Swindon, for instance, coal cost nearly 18s a ton, as
opposed to almost £2 a few years previously. Clothiers at Chippenham
evidently made use of this cheaper fuel, for several factories were
revitalised, and a new corn mill was built. But a long recession in the cloth
trade, beginning about 1816, meant there was very little economic growth
in the town until some time after the railway came through. Then several
small repair and metal forging shops opened up, including one owned by
Rowland Brotherhood, an associate of Brunel.

In 1848 Brotherhood established a railway works along the line at
Cocklebury. By 1853 it had become 'a large manufactory, with a steam
engine and iron foundry for the making of rails, trucks, and carriages for
the railway'. Three years later the firm had a contract with GWR to
undertake 'the repair and maintenance of the earth work and ballasting, the
permanent way, sidings, station buildings, bridges and viaducts, tunnels
and culverts, drains, level crossings, roads, fences and other works from
Reading to Bristol'. The contract continued for eight years and evidently
proved profitable, for another railway works was started by Brotherhood in
the Cocklebury area. Here new tracks, switches and other signalling
apparatus were to be made to replace those which had begun to wear out
along the line. It is likely that during the eight years Rowland Brotherhood
had also tackled the problem of slippage at the Cocklebury cutting, and
repaired its original ballasting. The contract also gave him another source of
income. He used the land along the line as grazing areas for cattle, and
made hay on the cuttings and embankments, which he offered for sale to
local farmers. A new access road built to Chippenham station from the
town decided Rowland Brotherhood to expand again. In his own words he
'bought a strip of land (part of Tynings field) by the site of the works
fronting the station at Chippenham and built a new shop for Peter [his son]
to make locomotive engines in'. By this time other small workshops had set
up nearby; Cocklebury's first industrial estate had been created.

An advertisement in the *Gazette* stated Brotherhood's manufactory,
besides making boilers, point work and signals, wagon and carriage
wheels, was also an agency for Silcocks agricultural machinery. In addition,
'Iron and Brass Castings' and 'General Smith's work' was carried out on the
premises. Rowland Brotherhood was an enterprising and imaginative
character. He once took a locomotive by road from Cocklebury to a new
branch line opening near Bristol, claiming the difficulties of taking it via the
main line were greater than taking it by road. The incident was, of course,
what would be called today a publicity stunt. Unfortunately, such business
flair was destined to be nipped in the bud, for, in rather strange

circumstances, the North Wiltshire Bank (of which one of the Goldney family was a director) foreclosed mortgages on him. Perhaps he had borrowed too heavily and was in serious debt. Rowland Brotherhood left Chippenham in 1872, to be heard of no more. A pity, for he was a colourful figure in the life of the town and brought great prosperity to it.

Brotherhood's engineering works, during the following 40 years, changed ownership several times. In 1920 Westinghouse Brake Company commenced manufacturing there. For many years Chippenham's largest employer, their engineering works and office buildings now cover much of the area of Cocklebury from Foundry Lane to Pew Hill. Since 1982, Westinghouse Brake and Signal Company Ltd. has consisted of six independent companies on the site, and is a member of the Hawker Siddeley Group.

In 1853 there was only a quarter of a mile between Brotherhood's works and Monkton House. The smoke and noise from the works, plus the growth of new dwellings in close vicinity of the House's driveway began to upset its owners. They felt their house was no longer a fit residence for a private family. So Esmeade's Estate Act was put before Parliament. It represented an effort by the family to break the conditions of their inheritance of the estate laid down by Anne Michell in her will, and recorded their desire to sell the land for building plots. Parliament, however, rejected the Act and the estate remained intact.

If the Act had been passed, it is interesting to consider whether the family would have been able to sell Monkton for building plots to Chippenham entrepreneurs. Probably not, for access to Monkton land–as it still is today–was blocked off by the river and hindered by the lack of major roads; so even if the land had been available the expansion of Chippenham would have continued exactly where it did, along the sides of the railway. What the Esmeade family probably had in mind, however, was to be able to sell the estate as a whole, for the middle of the 19th century was very similar to the time just before the Reformation, when there were many nouveau-riche merchants, well able to afford a small country estate, but finding very few properties available for purchase. By 1853, the Esmeades apparently wished to live in London. If they could have sold Monkton, the capital thus realised, placed in stocks or some similar investment, would have been far more convenient to manage than their country estate.

Anne Michell of Monkton House had died in 1844 and the estate had been inherited by a cousin, Graham Moore. At the time of her marriage to Edward Michell in 1833, she had had a settlement executed to ensure that all of Monkton would go to her family intact in the event she died before her husband. Her will, written after her marriage, was even more specific.[2] She left the estate to her cousin, providing he took the name of Michell Esmeade, and resided at Monkton every year for at least four consecutive months. He was not to let the gardens or pleasure grounds (thereby guaranteeing their upkeep as such?), and leasing terms of the farmland at Cocklebury were set forth. Other clauses specified that £15,000 of 3%

consuls were to be invested in land or estate, ten guineas a year to be provided for dinner and wine for the jurors and officials of the manor court, and several generous annuities and bequests were to be made to her household servants. This will left little option for Graham Moore but to abide by its terms; evidently Anne had realised that his interest in Monkton was less than hers (as the later presentation of the Estate Act to Parliament was to prove), and so she made sure by all the legal means at her command that the estate would remain intact within the family. Graham's brother, who inherited after him, retained his own name. He was also able to circumvent the residential clause of Anne's will, for he rented Monkton House and ground to the Awdry family, and lived in London at Eaton Square. After his death at the end of the 19th century, his only daughter, Mary Carrick Moore, inherited. She always lived in London, and sold Monkton in 1919.

The diarist, the Reverend Francis Kilvert, who lived for part of his life at Langley Burrell, knew Monkton well, for he was a good friend of the Awdry family. He also walked through Cocklebury on his frequent journeys to and from Chippenham station. He had another reason to go to Cocklebury, for as part of Langley Burrell parish, he visited parishioners living there. His diaries are a mine of information for any local historian interested in rural life in the 1800s. He was able to communicate with people of all classes and convey to his readers their way of life. If he had a flaw, it was his acceptance of the endless drudgery of farm work, and the poverty due to inadequate wages, which the labourers of his day had to endure. But he lived in a time when few people recognised this situation, and if they did, they felt there was little they could do to alleviate it or its causes, especially in the depths of the Wiltshire countryside, except to provide charity. Kilvert's virtues far outweighed his faults. He perceived his world as a gentle world, he saw the best in people, and he gave them his best. Through his love for the countryside and its people, and his gift for words, he has made his world live for his readers today. 'How delicious to get into the country again, the sweet damp air and scent of the beanfields. I do loathe London.' 'I walked up by Cocklebury, the lanes and fields deliciously shady green and quiet.' He was extremely sensitive to sounds: 'Across the great level meads near Chippenham came the martial music of a drum and fife and the laughing voices of unseen girls were wafted from the farm and hayfields out of the wide dusk'. 'At five minutes to midnight the bells of Chippenham church pealed out loud and clear in the frosty air'.

He was often at Monkton House with his sister, Fanny, for croquet, an archery party, a dinner or just a visit. But he did not neglect seeing his parishioners at Cocklebury. He called it 'villaging'. He often had tea with the Matthews family at Rawlings and in his diary relates the involvement of John Matthews in the notorious fight between men of Chippenham and Langley Burrell in 1822. John was 'old Father Matthews' by Kilvert's time, and he once described him as 'sitting in the corner by the fire with his white smock frock and innocent rosy childlike face'. A long time from John's fighting days! The fight was a culmination of a lengthy rivalry, and began at Chippenham Clift. It ended up near the middle of the town, and in the course of the fight, several men were killed. With others involved, John was afterwards taken to a public house and chained to a long iron bar, for there was no jail in Chippenham. Sixteen of the offenders were eventually tried at Salisbury. Anthony Guy and Edward Michell acted for the Prosecution. John made a confession and he was not accused of murder. He went to prison, but for how long has not been discovered.

In 1874, Kilvert talked to old Mrs. Matthews about a great number of railway accidents occurring at the time. 'It's shocking to be ushered out of the world in that way', she commented. Two years later he had to comfort both the old people for the loss of their son, 'staff of their old age' who had died after four months of illness. But the family did not have to leave Rawlings, for Harriet and Alice Matthews (their daughters?) assumed the tenancy.

A great storm hit the area in 1872, 'the whole world seemed to be groaning and straining under the press of . . . dreadful wind' throughout an evening and night. The damage done was considerable; 'an elm fell at Cocklebury and crushed a cow to death. The Awdrys at Monkton were sitting around the drawing room fire when the chimney stack fell, the bricks, stones and mortar came thundering down the chimney and drove the fire and soot and dust and ashes all over the room, damaging the furniture and carpet considerably'.

During a visit to Patience Ferris at Cocklebury Cottage, Kilvert was told the story of a mysterious burial by a man and a boy near the railway, which her son Jacob had witnessed. Later the same day, after he had finished his work at Rawlings, Jacob, with another lad from the farm, decided to dig up the box, hoping to find money. But inside there was only a damp smelly parcel. They left it unopened and told Jacob's father. He examined it, likewise left it unopened, and sent for the Chippenham policeman. Before the policeman arrived, a neighbour, with fewer inhibitions, found the box and noticed on the lid was written 'Goodbye, poor Bunny, 1876'. Jacob Ferris (who along with his father and the other farm boy undoubtedly could not read) had to endure much teasing and comment from his friends. Unkindly, they also called out after him the inscription on the box. This little story has its parallel in the fable of the Wiltshire moonrakers, who, when encountering excise men on a moonlight night, threw their kegs of brandy into a nearby pond and explained they were raking for the cheese they could see. But in that story it was authority that was made fun of, not the country lads.

From Kilvert's descriptions of Cocklebury it is obvious that the number of people living there towards the end of the 19th century had declined to the point where it was a very small community. But its separate identity still remained and was to do so for many years.

The drop in population at Cocklebury in the 19th century was chiefly due to the decline in the number of cottages there. The wattle and daub or timber dwellings remaining from the previous century gradually fell into disrepair, and becoming unfit to live in, were abandoned or pulled down. The need for housing in the area is reflected in the 1841 census, when the number of people living in barns and tents were listed as follows: Calne 11, Chippenham 45, Corsham 6, and Langley Burrell 18. But it did not pay either a landlord or his tenant to build workers' cottages, for the low wages of the times prevented any payment of a rent providing a reasonable return on the costs of construction. It was not until 1870 or so that four well-built stone cottages were provided at Cocklebury by the Monkton estate. But there was never to be enough accommodation for workers until after the Second World War, when mechanisation replaced so many workers on the farm.

Lack of housing during much of the 19th century was not the only burden suffered by the agricultural labourer at Cocklebury. Equally heavy were the extremely low rates of pay, for a work week of seldom less than 70 hours. An example of poverty at the time, Kilvert cites the example of John Hattherell, working for the Langley Burrell estate, who remembered 50 years later that in 1823 he could not afford to buy enough bread to feed all his family, so he sacrificed his own share to his children. Such a story is repeated over and over again in local records and confirmed by a Commission appointed by Parliament in 1843 to enquire into working conditions of women and children in agriculture.

One of the towns where the Commission received evidence was Calne, and of the workers interviewed, several were employed on dairy farms near Cocklebury. The evidence presented proved conclusively that the agricultural labourer in the area was just as badly off as John Hattherell was 20 years before. The Commissioners were told of wages of 8s a week for men, 4s a week for women, and a few pennies for children depending on their age. These wages provided rent, barely enough food and a few clothes. Fuel was usually gathered from hedgerows or woods. Most families lived in one- or two-bedroom cottages, sometimes two families in one cottage (at Studley there were 29 persons in one cottage, but this was an extreme case). The typical cottage was always damp from lack of proper drainage and wet seeping through the clay or flagstone floor.

'There is never enough to eat' was the theme of the evidence presented to the Commissioners. This was not because of lack of food produced in the area, but because wages were so low that only a little meat or pigs' offal could be purchased once a week, in addition to small amounts of butter, tea and sugar. These were used to supplement meals consisting of bread, potatoes and cabbage–these vegetables were usually grown in an allotment supplied by their employer or village.

Assistance had to be obtained for clothes, bedding, and any difficult circumstances, such as a crippled child in the family, who could not be sent out to earn a few pence. People were willing to work, and to walk many miles to their place of employment, but it was impossible to find a wage adequate to support a family. A doctor giving evidence considered the inevitable deterioration of health that occurred early in women agricultural workers was due to their long hours of work, their poor food, and their inability to change out of damp clothes, rather than to the actual work they did on the farm. The exception to this was dairy work, which, as cheeses were now being made up to 50 lbs in weight, was considered too hard for women.

The Commission made no comment on evidence presented indicating how a woman had to get up before her family to prepare a fire to boil water on, so they could at least have a hot drink before going out to work. There was not enough time to furnish a breakfast even if suitable food to cook had been available, so bread and perhaps a little bacon or cheese was taken for food for the day. After her work was done, usually at dusk, a woman then had to walk home, perhaps several miles, and set to preparing an evening meal. Her labour was ceaseless, her only rest when she slept. For much of her working life, she was pregnant, so it is little wonder the Commission seldom found employed women in good health over the age of forty.

To alleviate the distress of the women agricultural labourers, the consensus of opinion of the educated witnesses heard at Calne (these included the doctor, a clergyman and a local business man) was that emigration should be encouraged, and more badly-drained land should be brought into production to provide more jobs and more food, hence lowering prices. No mention was made of lessening hours of work, or of increasing rates of pay. It took 40 years before either began to occur, and then only because of a labour shortage in rural areas, the struggles of a badly-supported union movement and the attitude of a few liberal politicians such as Joseph Collins.

Personal recollections told to the author by farm workers born in the last half of the 19th century indicate that there was no tradition of women working in the fields–except at hay making and harvest time–in the Chippenham area throughout the period of this chapter. Kilvert's diary bears this out, though in his time women continued to make cheese and work in the dairy. So, unless she was a dairymaid, the lot of a woman married to a labourer at Cocklebury was perhaps a little easier than a woman who worked outside in other areas. Certainly if she was home most of the day a better family life could be attained, but it would be achieved at the loss of her earnings to the family's budget.

The low and inadequate wages can be blamed to a great extent on two factors; the attitude of employers to their workers, and the Poor Law system. The employer paid the lowest wage the current market for labour would bear, and considered the labourer should be thankful that he had a

job with so much unemployment in the Chippenham area. The idea of
raising wages was an unknown concept, and furthermore, it was not
considered necessary, for until 1834, when the Poor Law system was
abolished, supplements were provided to inadequate wages.

A farmer was assessed at certain intervals by his parish for the level of
rate he should pay to provide funds for the relief of the poor, whether
employed or not. The system's laws made provision for the money raised
by these rates to be paid to the poor or workers in need, the amount based
on the current price of wheat (and hence bread). Because of the existence of
these wage supplements, a farmer naturally paid the lowest possible wage
tolerated by the workers. As the Parliamentary enquiry revealed, the actual
wage paid did not cover even the bare essentials of life, and to obtain such
necessities as clothing, bedding, fuel, and the tools needed for work,
application had to be made to parish relief officers. A degrading experience,
but so common that little was thought of it by the employers, and nobody
cared how the worker felt about it.

By the end of the 1840s, the situation had begun to change in the
Chippenham area. The farmer was reluctantly beginning to accept the fact
that he had to pay a living wage (only a matter of a few shillings); there was
less unemployment as the new jobs had been created on the railway and in
the new engineering works; and emigration overseas had started. All these
factors combined to edge agricultural wages up, though very slowly.
Another relief at the time to the labourer was a considerable decrease in the
price of bread, due to imported wheat. Later meat and cheese from
overseas began to enter the county in large quantities, and by 1870 the
purchasing power of a worker's weekly wage had increased by 60 per cent.

The lot of a worker at Cocklebury after the 1870s had improved. He
had a new cottage to live in, and he was being paid more (though there
were eight disastrous farming years in the 1880s when he voluntarily
accepted a reduction in pay), and by the end of the century, with
perquisites such as an allotment and free milk, his wage was nearly a
pound a week. His job was secured by the shortage of farm labour in other
parts of the county. But there was still no pension when he was too old to
work, and he then had to depend on his family, or charity, or the
Chippenham workhouse to provide him and his wife with a roof. So
although his working years had improved, in his old age he was no happier
or better off than his father or grandfather before him.

If the agricultural worker at Cocklebury endured an uncertain fortune
in the 19th century, the life of the farmers there during the same time can be
summed up in one word–stability. This stability was assured by three
keystones: the security of tenure offered him by the long leases of both
Langley Burrell and Monkton manors; the regular income derived from the
sales of his cheese and later his liquid milk; and the profits from the sales of
grazing stock and pigs–'the gentlemen who pay the rent'.

The railway proved to be of great economic benefit to the farmer at Cocklebury. It enabled him to take advantage of lower transportation costs to bring in greater amounts of goods which were considered by the mid-century to be basic to the needs of farming–cotton seed oil cake for cattle feed, bone dust, guano and phosphates for additional fertilization of his land, and tiles for drainage. Later, the railway provided the opportunity to transport milk to London, a far more profitable and less laborious way to market milk than to turn it into cheese.

A Vale farmer had no difficulty in obtaining labour through most of the century. As has been related, until the 1850s there were plenty of men and women desperately in need of a job, who cost little to hire and could literally be worked from dawn to dusk. Only one protest in the Vale against such harsh working conditions has so far been discovered.[3] Even the famous Captain Swing movement of the 1830s did not reach the claylands of the Vale.[4] The docility of the farmworker, always a concern of farmers at the Chippenham Agricultural Association meetings evidently continued for most of the century. Kilvert mentions it in his diaries, and Trade Union workers made very little headway in organising the area.

Henry White, a tenant at Cocklebury in the 1880s, did not have to worry about his labour. One of his employees was awarded a prize by he CAA for 34 years of 'servitude' (here used in a vastly different sense than that of today) and he constantly won prizes for cheese making; evidently he was able to obtain and to keep good workers.

What sort of persons were the farmers at Cocklebury in the second half of the 19th century–Richard Rich, Henry White and the Matthews family? Their greatest interest lay in the land they farmed, it would certainly have formed the basis of their lives. Like their landlords, they too were conservative in politics and in their general outlook on the world. They probably had little vision of any social or economic changes affecting their lives, but they kept up with innovations and changes in the pattern of farming.

Richard Rich was a man of public service who gave generously of his time. He was elected to the Chippenham Borough Council, and became Mayor in 1870. With Edward Little of Sheldon and others he was a founder of the CAA. He entered his cattle and horses from Cocklebury at the Association's annual shows for many years, but he seldom won a prize. Henry White took over the tenancy of Cocklebury farm in the early 1880s. He had better luck than Richard Rich at shows, for he entered his Wiltshire cheeses and won prizes year after year. Unfortunately, although little else has been discovered about him, he was, no doubt, a steady, able, honest, hard-working farmer of the Vale. The Matthews family did not, however, apparently participate in the social life of Chippenham. Kilvert conveys the impression that they were a family who kept much to themselves. It is likely their social activities lay chiefly with their many relatives who lived near them, at Hardenhuish and Langley Burrell. All these people were worthy citizens, their place in their society was assured. None of them sought what is called by sociologists today 'upward mobility'.

In agriculture at Cocklebury in the 19th century basically the same processes were taking place that had prevailed for hundreds of years. Food for man and animals was grown and taken from the land; the land was refertilized and the cycle began again. Now there was a difference, however. By drainage and extra fertilizing, the land was being stimulated to produce heavier crops. This stimulation was a form of improvement to the land and in time posed a vexing question to the farming world of England and finally to a Parliamentary Commission–how could the person who carried out the extra fertilizing and drainage benefit fully from these procedures? In the case of the tenant, he had to be sure that his lease was long enough to give him time to cover his investment. The landlord, if he paid for drainage, was concerned with a rent rise, and whether his tenant would adjust his methods of farming accordingly. If they mutually agreed to share the costs, and the lease was extended for a period long enough for the farmer to recover his share of the expenditure, then all was well. If no agreement existed, which was frequently the case, either the tenant or the landlord sustained a loss. At Cocklebury, with the long tenancies there, disputes on this difficult question were apparently amicably settled and cultivation of the land proceeded on his unhurried way. The better drainage and greater manuring of the fields must certainly have changed their appearance. They were dryer for most of the year, the grass less rank and much greener.

New breeds of animals were introduced during the century. The popular Longhorn cattle were supplanted by Shorthorns, to remain at Cocklebury and many other farms in the Vale until the 1940s, when Friesians began to replace them. Mr. Little, the farmer at Sheldon, wrote in 1844 that though most local herds had almost pure bred animals, some Shorthorns were crossed with Ayrshire or Gloucester–to improve the richness of the milk–or with Hereford to make a better beef animal. The old Wiltshire horned sheep had quite disappeared, and a cross between Cotswold and South Down was common in the Chippenham area, probably producing a dual purpose animal with a good fleece and a slightly heavier, more compact carcase. There is no doubt that sheep still played an important role in the economy of a Vale farm in the first half of the 19th century. The new favourite breed of pig was the Spotted or the Berkshire, but later the Berkshire was crossed with a Wiltshire White to develop a pig suitable for the bacon market of the time.

In the area of cropping, the fallow year had been replaced in the cycle by a nitrogenous crop; at Cocklebury the cycle no doubt consisted of beans, followed by wheat or another corn or root crop, then clover or french, and sometimes rye.

The more complex demands of pastoral farming and its smaller fields, combined with an abundance of cheap labour, slowed the adoption of machinery. By the middle of the century, however, seed drills for turnips, clover and other such crops had appeared, and a threshing machine and its crew visited the farms if the amount of corn grown justified it. Cake cutters (oil cake for the cattle came in large slabs) and turnip choppers were other labour-saving devices that had reached Cocklebury. The hard work of hay making had been lightened by the invention of a mower, swathe turner, tedder, and mechanical rack. All were drawn by horses, for it was many years after the 19th century before Cocklebury saw its first tractor, or is first hay elevator, powered by a small puttering diesel engine, to convey hay from carts in which it was collected to the rick or barn.

The household tasks of brewing, baking and bacon salting no longer existed, but cider making continued, utilizing apples from the orchards around Cocklebury farm. Perry may have been made at Rawlings, for a huge ancient pear tree was in existence at the back of the farmhouse until fairly recently. A stone from Cocklebury farm's cider press survives today.

Until 1860 or so, milk produced at Cocklebury had always been used for cheese making. Before the advent of the railways, the market for liquid milk had been of little commercial significance outside the cities. As early as 1847, however, milk was being shipped to Liverpool from Cheshire farms, and by 1866 over seven million gallons had been shipped to London from GWR stations as far away as below Swindon. It is difficult to pinpoint the exact date milk from Cocklebury began to go to London, for detailed freight records of the GWR are lacking before 1866, but the nearness of the farms to the station, the greater profitability of liquid milk, and the ease of change (all that was needed were churns, for at first the milk went uncooled) probably prompted the switch as soon as milk trains began to run to Paddington from Chippenham station.

To send the unprocessed milk from the farm must have had a revolutionary effect on its routine–as great as the introduction of the milking machine in the next century. The daily tasks of cheese making, all the anxieties concerning its quality, and the long wait between production of the milk and sale of the cheese were suddenly ended. Instead, the milk was put into churns, and taken by horse and wagon to the station to be transported to London by train.

The churns holding the milk may have been manufactured by the forerunner of Spencers at Melksham, John Gillet. The farmer had to have several sets of them, as the empties were not always sent back down the line from Paddington the same day. And when they were returned, there was the work of cleaning them thoroughly, for an empty milk churn standing in hot sun or being delayed on its return to the farm would soon turn sour. The churns were conical in shape, about 3 ft. 6 ins. high, and held 17 gallons of milk. A brass plate with the farmer's name on it was riveted onto the churn for identification. Some of these churns dating back 50 years were still in use at Cocklebury in the 1940s. When full they were very heavy to handle and it took two men to lift them into the milk wagon.

But empty, their height and shape made them easy to roll on their bottom rim, and the author became very proud of her dexterity in this skill!

The last quarter of the century were difficult years for the farmers at Cocklebury. There were bad summers between 1874 and 1882. As the *Gazette* commented 'summers with no warm weather'. Milk yields were lowered, and the cheese market was badly hit by the large amount of cheap cheese imported from North America. The farms were threatened with foot and mouth disease (though there was no indication that it reached Cocklebury, and so far as is known an outbreak of the dreaded disease has never occurred there), and swine fever lingered in the area. More foreign competition from meat produced overseas lowered prices for fat cattle. Many farm sales were reported in the Chippenham area. Adjoining Cocklebury, Peckingell farm went up for sale in 1876 and again in 1881, but no change of tenancy, except for reasons of death or retirement, happened at Cocklebury.

On the brighter side, Chippenham Horticultural Society held its show in the grounds of Monkton House for many years. These shows began a tradition which continues to the present day. For many years the annual Chippenham Horse and Flower Show (of which the Horticultural Show was the forerunner) took place at Cocklebury. Fun fairs were set up in Green Ditch field, and more recently festivities have frequently been held in Monkton Park.

Those living at Cocklebury in 1900 in essence consisted of several isolated units, the people of the two farms and residents of Avon, Monkton and Pew Hill Houses. The position of the manor lord or squire as a patriarch had long since ended, but a social structure remained. At the top were the people of the houses; then came the farmers, and finally the workers. The farms were in good order, the current scarcity of labour not affecting Cocklebury. As workers told the author, a job there was always worth having, for it was so near to Chippenham and its amenities.

Chapter Nine

The Twentieth Century at Cocklebury

Another turning point in the story of Cocklebury took place in the 20th century, when the chief use of its land changed from agriculture to the provision of sites for housing and industry. Cocklebury had, of course, ceased to be purely a farming area by the late 1840s. Over the years to 1900 a bacon and a cheese factory, and more engineering works and foundries clustered around Foundry Lane, and towards Pew Hill several rows of terraced houses were about to be built. This industrial growth at Cocklebury provided jobs, goods and services for the ever-growing population, and their value exceeded many times the value of the agricultural produce of Cocklebury and Rawlings farms.

Thirty years of depressed prices and a shortage of capital made the start of the new century a difficult time for English farmers. However, Henry White at Cocklebury farm, and the new tenant who had replaced the Matthews family at Rawlings were able to keep their land in good order. Both farms concentrated on milk production. The market for liquid milk continued to expand due to the increase in population and changing patterns of food consumption. Both factors meant a greater use of milk. There were several markets for milk from Cocklebury in 1900. It could be shipped by rail from Chippenham station to London; taken to Nestles milk factory, manufacturing condensed milk in Chippenham; or used by the cheese factory at Foundry Lane, recently started by local business men to produce Cheddar cheese. The best price a farmer could obtain for his milk came from shipping it to London. Cocklebury farm had done this for several decades, and in all likelihood Rawlings did as well. But in the late spring months, a time of surplus, extra milk could be taken to the cheese factory. Many English farmers at the time not only operated at a loss, but also were not able to maintain the level of output and fertility of their farms.

White and Harding, however, were able to sell all the milk they produced and besides make a return on the labour and investment they put into their farms.

In 1912, Henry White left Cocklebury farm. The tenancy was taken over by James Miller, who stayed there seven years. His lease survives, and it emphasises, in a mixture of old and new clauses, the essential need, always present since farming began at Cocklebury to keep the land in good heart and to ensure its continuing productivity. This 1912 lease specified the rent of Cocklebury farm as £420 a year, or approximately £2 an acre, an average figure for the area at the time. As was usual, the lease begins with the right of the landlord to all hunting, shooting and fishing on the farm, to all trees (with their 'lops, tops and shrouds', and to wood, quarries, mines, stone gravel, sand, clay, brick, earth and other minerals. The tenant was obliged to keep fences, hedges and ditches in good order and to be allowed 'sufficient rough timber' to do so, a privilege going back many centuries.

Because corn crops take so much fertility from the land, it is not surprising, though Cocklebury was at the time all pasture and meadow-land, that the lease specified in great detail the question of the frequency of their cultivation and rotation with other crops. There was even a heavy penalty clause stating if the tenant ploughed up pasture to grow corn crops without the permission of the landlord he could be fined £50 per acre. But the crux of the lease was to ensure that if anything was taken from the land, it was to be returned, albeit in another form. Hence the stringent conditions, not only on the growing of corn crops, but on the number of hay crops that could be taken from the farm's fields every year, and the removal of any hay, straw, or manure from the farm. If hay or straw was removed without the landlord's permission, for each ton taken, three tons of manure or 30s-worth of artificial fertilizer was to be purchased and used on the land. The tenant was also admonished that for any milk produced for sale, he should return 'such an amount of manure as shall suffice to prevent any impoverishment of the land'.

Clauses such as those just described were no doubt copied from previous leases (and in the case of the monetary value of artificial fertilizer, updated), as was one showing the importance placed on the farm's ability to make cider; a damaged tree producing the fruit for the cider was to be replaced by 'a thriving young apple tree'. Other clauses included strictures that molehills and ant-hills were to be dug up and 'spread abroad', and that the tenant was 'to use his best endeavours to keep the premises free from thistles, docks, briers, furze and noxious weeds'.

James Miller farmed Cocklebury during the years of the First World War. The acreage of pasture and meadowland remained the same then, unlike the Second World War. Probably the only change to take place was an increase in the number of beef cattle and pigs raised, and the amount of potatoes grown.

Meanwhile, more land at Cocklebury had been utilized for urban needs. Chippenham and District County School was built opposite the station; in time a playing field was to be added, partly carved out of Tinings field. All this area is now utilised for the buildings of Chippenham Technical College. On the other side of the school, Wiltshire Farmers Limited bought land for a creamery, and an oil depot was established at Cocklebury just beyond the station.

In 1919, Mary Carrick Moore, now a very old lady, decided to sell all the Monkton estate and so severed the tie her family had had with the area for more than two centuries. The estate was bought by a farmer from Somerset, Charles Tucker. He immediately sold Monkton House and gardens to its tenant, and later, some of the fields around Pew Hill House, which were purchased by the House's owner. Cocklebury farm itself was now 200 acres or so, and was to be farmed by Charles Tucker's daughter, aged 19 at the time of the sale. She managed it for seven years, until her marriage to Edwin Self of Lacock. (The Selfs are probably of Saxon origin, for their name has appeared continually in documents of north-west Wiltshire since the beginning of written records in Norman times.)

Soon after their marriage, Mr. and Mrs. Self modernized Cocklebury farmhouse. They installed running water and electricity, and built a second staircase in the house by replacing a ladder in the north-east corner of its original section. A bathroom was installed, and the kitchen newly equipped. The oldest chimney in the house also needed attention, so it was relined. While this work was being done, much of the original clay lining of the flue was discovered adhering to the surrounding stone walls, still in good condition after more than 300 years of continuous use.

The early 1930s were a time of worldwide economic depression. In England, it affected agriculture throughout the country. The Vale farmers were a little better off than many others, for they were always able to sell their milk and to make ends meet. The Selfs continued to farm at Cocklebury. When asked by the author to describe the Depression, they summed it up in one sentence: 'life went on much the same, we had the monthly milk check and we lived very carefully'.

After these years several more buildings appeared along the road by the station, but the land that was built on had not been used for farming for quite a while, so there was technically no loss of farmland from Cocklebury. Thereafter, no more building was to take place on the eastern side of the railway until the 1950s. The *Gazette*, at the time of the sale of Monkton, had anticipated that the land between the station and Monkton House was 'ripe for development' and that Chippenham could now 'expand in the right direction'. The implied prediction proved false, for the town had enough building land more conveniently located to provide for its needs until after the Second World War.

In 1938 the tenancy of Rawlings farm became vacant. It was taken over by Mr. Self, and for the next 30 years Rawlings and Cocklebury, comprising

320 acres, were run as one farm. The only exception involved the dairy cattle, which were retained as two herds of milking cows with their young stock. They were kept separately at each farm, one herd being grazed and milked at Cocklebury, the other at Rawlings. Sheep had begun to be kept again by the Selfs, a cross-breed of Border Leicester and Hampshire Down. Just before the Second World War Mr. Self bought a few Cheviots which 'he liked the look of'. But they were not a happy choice, for Cheviots are a breed of sheep that are used to unconfined hill grazing, and Cocklebury's fields did not suit them. 'They broke out of every field we put them in, we had to sell them eventually, they tried our patience too much!' By 1941, however, all the sheep at Cocklebury were gone; they took too much out of land that produced more, and did not become so depleted, if it was grazed by dairy cattle. The number of pigs at Cocklebury had also been reduced, chiefly because it was difficult to make a profit on them.

As in other major wars, the years 1939-1945 saw an increase in the production of food at Cocklebury. They also brought with them another turning point in Cocklebury's history, for they speeded the trend towards comprehensive mechanisation of the work of the farm. The process was slow, however. At the outbreak of the war, all the farm machinery, such as the hay-making equipment, the drills and harrows, and the carts and wagons, were pulled by horses. There was an old tractor, used for moving the hay elevator and other heavy jobs, and a milking machine. This had been abandoned when the Selfs returned to hand milking again, after they had demonstrated that it gave higher milk yields. Ten years later, in 1949, there were four tractors. All the horses had gone. The Shorthorn cows had been replaced by higher-yielding pedigree Friesians, milked by machines. Cocklebury had become mechanised.

The needs of war, and the advice of the Wiltshire Agricultural Advisory Committee, resulted in some fields at Cocklebury being ploughed after 100 years or more of having been laid down to pasture. The ploughing released a considerable amount of latent fertility of the soils beneath the pastures, and the crops grown in these fields were abundant. Green Ditch, partially on the Cornbrash, produced 15 sacks to the acre when its first crop of wheat was harvested, a result that gave pride to everyone on the farm. A crop newly introduced to Cocklebury–sugar beet–also produced record yields. Many acres of potatoes were grown, to be harvested by school children, housewives, and even gangs of German prisoners-of-war.

By careful feeding and a new recording scheme, milk production during the war years at Cocklebury increased, and poor-yielding cows were culled from its two herds. To supplement the hay and imported oilcake fed to the cows in the winter, the farm grew extra kale and root crops. Silage, another supplement, which was made for the first time in 1942, was initially not a great success until the intricacies of its making were better understood.

Sometime during the autumn months of the war years came the threshing machine with its crew of two men and four land girls. From the taking of the sheaves off the ricks to be pitch-forked into the whirling maw of the machine to the wheeling away of the heavy sacks of grain (especially if the grain was wheat), this was a dusty job and hard work for everyone. As the rick became low, a chicken-wire fence was unrolled and placed around it. Everyone in the area who had a dog stood by, and as the bottom two or three layers of sheaves began to be moved, the rats and mice left the rick. The place became bedlam, men shouting and dogs barking. Not until the last rat was killed by the dogs or clubbed to death did the noise stop. Though this would be considered barbaric by many people today, at the time it all seemed very exciting.

No bombs were dropped at Cocklebury during the war; but in 1943, an RAF Mosquito plane crashed on to Rawlings farmhouse. Both the pilot and co-pilot were instantly killed, and so was the tenant of the farmhouse, who was trapped by fire and falling timber beams. The author happened to witness the crash, and can still recall the uncanny way in which the plane, as it fell out of the sky, seemed drawn towards the farmhouse which was the only building within a quarter-mile radius. Oddly enough, a plane crash had also occurred at Cocklebury in the First World War, but it has thus far proved impossible to discover any further details about the incident. The chance of two crashes occurring in such an area surely must be very slender.

Compared to the arrival of railway navvies working at Cocklebury just a hundred years before, the invasion of American troops in the Chippenham area in 1944 was far more welcome. Many of the soldiers came from rural backgrounds, and found their way from the town to Cocklebury, to ask for a glass of fresh milk, or just to enjoy the farm atmosphere. To the delight of local small boys, several hundred soldiers camped in Monkton Park for a week or so, in preparation for the invasion of Southern France. One summer's morning they had gone to join the war and the farm returned to its more peaceful but less exciting way of life.

Everyone on the farm was tired at the end of the war. It had been six years of hard work, despite plenty of available labour.[1] The most important product of the farm again became milk, and life revolved around the raising of young stock and beef cattle. Gradually the number of men working at Cocklebury became fewer, until only four were employed there in 1950. From the recollections of farm workers told to the author in the 1940s, it is apparent that they, like their fathers and grandfathers before them, were reluctant to sever their ties with the land, notwithstanding the hard and tedious nature of their work. Rates of pay were low, working hours were long and housing standards poor. There was little or no opportunity for advancement, and the status and prestige of farm workers was as low as always. Nevertheless, these factors did not deter them from continuing the traditional work of their families. Aubrey observed in the 17th century that the men of North Wiltshire were 'contemplative and melancholy'. In the 1940s his observation still applied to farm workers, and it can be added, they were somewhat quiescent and fatalistic in outlook. Thus they stayed on the land at Cocklebury until it could no longer employ them. It is probable that by the end of this century, the trials and tribulations, as well as the happier moments of their life and work will be quite forgotten, as the agricultural worker now holds, and rightly so, similar status, work and living conditions as any other worker.

Through the 1950s more Cocklebury land was taken for different needs. Westinghouse Brake & Signal Company purchased over thirty acres at Pew Hill. Chippenham cattle market moved from its location in the centre of the town to a site between the railway and Cocklebury farmhouse. At the same time, around Chippenham all available sites were being used for housing and other growth requirements. It began to be obvious that the next land to be taken for such use would be Cocklebury.

In 1957 120 acres of fields in the bend of the river at Monkton and Cocklebury were sold to provide a space for the increasing population of Chippenham. In the past 20 years, over 700 houses have sprung up there, plus a primary school, several shops, and an automobile showroom. On the edge of the estate lies Monkton Park, an open space created from the original parkland, and now in the possession of the people of Chippenham. Monkton House, within the Park's boundaries, is divided into flats. Behind the House is an old people's home. The Park is delightful. It is pleasant to walk there along the river, to play miniature golf, or, on a sunny day, just to sit, perhaps watching the little boats sail along the river. A large heated pool in the Park has replaced the river swimming facilities that were for over half a century offered at the old Bathing Place opposite Cocklebury land in the bend of the river there. These are now the headquarters of a Sea Scouts troops and a sailing club.

Although the major part of Cocklebury farm had been sold, the Selfs continued their interest in farming, for they retained the farmhouse, its buildings and 30 acres of the farm's land, running them, as had been done for 20 years, in conjunction with Rawlings. In 1963, their son took over the tenancy of Rawlings, and the Selfs gradually retired from farming. Cocklebury farmhouse stood empty for several years before being sold.

For a time the house was threatened by demolition, as it might have stood in the way of a new road planners were considering. This, however, has never materialised. The new owner, who wished to save the farmhouse, decided to seek a Grade II listing for it. This was easily obtained, as the house's historic merit as a fine example of a vernacular building was by then already realised. Being on the edge of the new housing estate, it seemed ideally suited for conversion into a public house. After some opposition, permission for such a use was granted by the local authorities.

Here, unfortunately, the fate of Cocklebury farmhouse has rested for several years. A buyer for it has yet to be found, for agreement cannot be reached with the North Wiltshire District Council on plans for development of the surrounding land, a little over two and a half acres. Having stood empty for so long, the farmhouse itself is in very poor condition and the out-buildings have been almost totally destroyed, having attracted the constant attention of vandals. The previous owner assured the author in 1980 that the house could be restored with little difficulty, for the walls and general structure are solid and well built, but it does not seem likely at the present time of writing that it will be allowed to survive.[2] So the present is reached in the Cocklebury story. Surrounded by housing and industry on three sides, Gordon Self runs Rawlings farm with one employee, maintaining a herd of beef Friesians, breeding and grazing Charolais cattle.

A new industrial estate is being built in the north-west corner of Cocklebury, eventually destined to cover over 35 acres of farmland. Planning permission for this estate was obtained more than ten years ago, but plans for development were not announced for several years. These plans were further delayed, because of the expense of providing roads and services to the area. In 1981 when the first building–a warehouse–was being erected, complaints of people living nearby revealed that the building had not been located in accordance with plans passed by the NWDC. Unfortunately construction was too far advanced to change the site. So the warehouse remains, far too visible and far too close to the main road and the surrounding houses. A year later local residents objected again, this time to the height of sections of a new factory. A committee of the NWDC insisted the sections be reduced from 23 to 15 metres. Residents' efforts this time had not been in vain.

At the time of writing (1982), further development at Cocklebury is restricted by the barrier of the railway lines, and lack of planning permission for its remaining agricultural land. But already future growth plans for Chippenham mention Rawlings farmland as a possible site for future housing. Farming at Rawlings is becoming more difficult. The acreage taken by Cocklebury Industrial Estate, and the demands and inconveniences of being next to an urban area affect the farm's integrity as a viable economic unit. To be there today has been aptly described by Mrs Gordon Self as living under siege conditions; 'one never knows if today will prove the day the farm has been approved for development'.

With the present trends towards urbanization around the town of Chippenham, the future of Cocklebury is not difficult to predict. The remaining farmland will sooner or later be used for housing and factory sites. If the money ever becomes available, a new highway will be built from Pew Hill to the Avon, to form a new link with the eastern outskirts of Chippenham, perhaps to become in time part of a ring road around the town.

Besides its historical content, this story has shown how 300 acres of prime farmland can disappear in less than a century (and half of that in the last 30 years) without comment or protest. It is a disappearance that has up to now been taken for granted, enabling society to provide for the economic, social and consumer needs of an expanding population. Today, however, these demands of a growth economy in England are competing with what is now considered another social need, the retention of the English countryside, a decision based at present mainly on aesthetic reasons. Up to now, growth needs have invariably won. No agricultural land on the edge of a city, town or village in England is safe from urban encroachment. If enough pressure is applied to the necessary governmental department, the land's designation can be altered, and a little later another few acres of agricultural land is lost for ever.

Since Saxon times, decisions affecting the use of land at Cocklebury (and for that matter in most parts of England) have always stemmed from political or economic motives. But these decisions were based on short term motives and had only short-term consequences. They were made with the consideration that more land was always available. Today this is no longer true. There is so little land left, the environmental dangers of paving it over are now well known, and people are waking up to the pros and cons of the argument of the value of open spaces and need for farmland versus the desire for economic growth.

The retention of the English countryside–or what is left of it–should now be the primary motive in all planning decisions, and political or economic needs should be made secondary. This may at first appear to be a biased statement. But, consider; with the continuing loss of agricultural land, what will happen when North Sea oil runs out and if the decline in exports fails to reverse itself? Then the country will run short of foreign exchange and will not be able to buy enough food–a commodity whose price is rapidly escalating in the world market. There will certainly never be enough land to supply all the food needed by England's population, but every acre producing food will release foreign exchange to bridge the gap in home and overseas supplies.

The author believes, after many years of participation in similar local planning decisions in the United States, that the time has come for local officials, in conjunction with central government departments and representatives of the public to sit down and devise a way that a line can be drawn around every city, town and village in England. Within the circle, development would be permitted. Without, the land would continue in agricultural use. At Cocklebury, as an example, such a line could be drawn along the railways, thus keeping the land attached to Rawlings farm. If that land goes before such a scheme materialised, why not draw a line along its 1000-year-old northern boundary, to last another millennium? The countryside is a legacy that must be left to future generations, to ensure that they too will be able to include it in their lives.

References

Chapter One
This chapter could not have been written without the help of two people; the late R. S. Barron, who took the time and interest to put me on the right geological tracks, and J. H. Tucker, an excellent guide to Stone Age activity at Cocklebury and in the Vale.

1. The three cultural groups were a) the Sauveterrains, who journeyed from France and Belgium to the Weald of Sussex around 8,500 BP, and then spread across to the west via the open dry chalk and limestone ridgeways; b) the Maglemosians, who arrived in Yorkshire from northern Europe about 10,000 BP, and who by their tools are known to have gradually moved south; and c) the Cheddarians, people who had long lived in the Cheddar area of the Mendips.

Chapter Two
1. I am indebted to Desmond J. Bonney of the Royal Commission on Historical Monuments, for his guidance and advice on the interpretation of the sparse knowledge at present available of the Saxon period in the Vale.
2. Much of the information on place-names in this chapter has been obtained from the publications, and from a personal communication, of Dr. Margaret Gelling. Any conclusions drawn are my own.
3. Aubrey's explanations on the origin of the name of Cocklebury which appear in his book, *Natural History of Wiltshire* (1847, reprinted Newton Abbot 1969) are observations based on supposition, viz: 'Cockleborough, near Chippenham, hath its denomination from the petrified cockles found there in great plenty, and as big as cockles'; and 'The rough stone about Chippenham (especially at Cockleborough) is full of petrified cockles': and so it may be, but Chippenham lies on the Cornbrash, Cocklebury on the Clays.
4. This explanation of a Saxon estate unit is quoted from an unpublished survey of the archaeology of the Chippenham area written in 1976 by W. J. Ford, former County Archaeological Officer for Wiltshire, and his staff.
5. Laws of King Ine. Concerning the rewards for tending pigs (see p. 00), this manorial custom bears a striking resemblance to law no. 49.3 (Whitelock 1979). Other similarities concern law no. 67, referring to payment for ploughing land, and perhaps no. 41 (of King Alfred) concerning recorded holdings of land.

Chapter Three
1. The text of Domesday Book has only once been printed, this was in 1783, in a limited edition of 1,250 copies, which are today extremely difficult to come by. Translations have been published, but many are out of print and others available only in large and costly volumes. By 1986 Phillimore & Co. will have published the first cheap and readily-available edition of the 18th-century printing, together with a parallel modern translation done to the highest academic standards.

2. Unless otherwise specified, information on local families and manorial customs of Chippenham has been taken from 13th- to 16th-century documents at the Public Record Office. They were translated by Mr. E. G. H. Kempson, and his transcriptions are in the possession of Mrs. Martin Gibbs of Sheldon Manor.

3. William le Oyselr. This name represents *Oliver*. It is variously spelt in other records as for instance, *Oly* and *Olyng*. Such variations are not unusual, for until the 18th century spelling was based on sound, preference and the hope of being understood!

Chapter Six

Much of the information on the woollen industry described in this chapter has been obtained from Mann (1974), Ramsey (1943) and Rogers (1976).

1. St Mary Street was in time to become the most fashionable street in Chippenham, and a profitable source of income to Monkton manor. Farleigh Priory had held much land there, so it was later acquired by the manor. As the street became fashionable, substantial houses built on manor land returned ground rents contributing to the manor's rent rolls.

2. 'Whitehouse'–usually the dairy. In the case of the Scott house, probably a larger dairy had been built and the old room was used for clothes washing and linen storage.

3. The Bakers were one of the first tenants to sign a lease with the newly-created Monkton manor. As small yeomen farmers, they leased land at Cocklebury for generation after generation. Their name disappears only when the last common field there was enclosed in the late 1700s, a time when it was becoming too difficult for one man to obtain a living from a dairy farm smaller than 30 acres.

4. Kilvert writes in 1874 of a very old man who remembered a cockpit and a bull ring at Langley Burrell. The bull ring was enclosed by a ditch and near common land. The old man could not recall seeing any cock fights or a bull being baited in his lifetime.

Chapter Seven

Agricultural information of north-west Wiltshire in the 18th century is taken chiefly from contemporary writers such as Thomas Davis, William Marshall and Arthur Young, and the modern writings of G. E. Fussell and R. Trow-Smith.

1. Annato is obtained from the seeds of a plant bearing the same name, powdered and compressed into a cake. It was not invented by Edgar Neale, a Chippenham chemist of the 19th century, as has been claimed. He discovered how to make it into a soluble solution, hence eliminating the difficulties powdered annato created–the variation in colour from one batch of cheese to another because the annato was hard to measure, and streaks or spots of colour which appeared in the cheese if the powder did not completely dissolve.

2. By 1733 the duties of a tythingman had probably been taken over by the Rector of Chippenham. The office of hayward had originated in the time of common fields, when it was necessary to supervise the care of fences and enclosures, impound stray cattle and oversee the husbandry of the fields. The breadweigher's duties were performed at Chippenham Market by an officer of the Borough.

3. The Reverend Ashe of Langley manor was billed £3 in 1829, by three men who took three poachers into custody and later to Corsham to be charged with their crime.

Chapter Eight

Besides Coleman (1968), MacDermott (1927), and VHW4, a major source of information on the GWR has been the company's records at the PRO.

1. After its construction the mean gradient of the line was 1 in 1,380, an achievement of engineering referred to as 'Brunel's billiard table'!

2. A detailed inventory of the contents of Monkton House at the time of Anne Michell's death indicate an extremely prosperous household, run in great elegance and style. Anne is a woman who deserves closer study, and there is plenty of material about her. She never stinted herself and her actions reveal the assurance of wealth.

3. Two meetings within a month of each other were held, at Goatacre and the nearby village of Bremhill in 1846. They were apparently organised by the labourers themselves and were reported in the national press. Hence the *Devizes Gazette* had to comment on them, albeit reluctantly, and did so, maligning the meetings' leaders. The paper also felt the need to be defensive, citing the large allocation of garden allotments to labourers in the district, and noting that despite the amount of unemployment in the area keeping wages low, all the protesters held jobs and should be thankful for them. Probably the starving unemployed were too weak to walk to the meetings!

4. 'Captain Swing' was a movement started by agricultural workers in 1830 in opposition to the threshing machine, which was considered a threat to their jobs. Many machines were destroyed, though none in the Vale, and some people were hurt, but no one killed. The riots, covering a period of two years, frightened the establishment, and consequently the perpetrators, if discovered, were severely punished by heavy fines, long imprisonment or transportation. The movement is probably the origin of the Chippenham Agricultural Association's perpetual concern with the 'docility' of the farm workers of the Vale.

Chapter Nine

1. The labour force at Cocklebury during the war years included Mr. and Mrs. Self, eight or nine agricultual workers, two Italian prisoners of war (they stayed nearly three years and for some of the time lived at the farmhouse), the author, and a maid (also living at the farmhouse). Several men from Chippenham provided casual, but skilled labour, in the evenings, weekends, hay making and harvest times. One of these men was responsible for thatching the ricks on the farm.

2. As this book goes to press, Cocklebury farmhouse presents a sorry spectacle, so systematically vandalised and neglected (despite its Grade 2 status) that it would almost appear to be the victim of a deliberate attempt to obliterate it. Will the publication of Cocklebury's story also mark the end of its long history?

Glossary

Alehouse: A house brewing its own ale and beer on the premises and not licensed to sell wine.

BP: Before present–i.e. BC plus 1980 years.

Buttery: A cool room for keeping milk, cream and butter, ale and beer.

Card: To card wool involved placing it between boards inserted with wire nails. The wool was pulled through the nails and untangled itself.

Demesne: The land nearest a Saxon estate or manor house, reserved for the use of the lord; later the 'home farm' of a manor or religious house.

Detached meadowland: In the Vale area, these are meadows producing good hay crops, lying chiefly on low grounds near rivers and streams. Many communities lacked such meadowlands, and were not able to obtain the hay needed for cattle to survive through the winter. Portions of meadowland were allocated to these communities, and they often lay several miles away. When parishes were created, the detached meadowland belonging to the community within the new parish was considered a part of the parish and the rights of use of the land continued. These rights were frequently retained until the 19th century. (Note: This definition has been supplied by W. J. Ford.)

Dress: To trim and align a cloth after dying.

Drugget: A heavy wool material, felted, rather like serge or twill. Made in the Devizes area in the 17th and 18th centuries.

Estate: For lack of a better word, this term has been used to describe a large Saxon landholding. Dr. Jan Titow considers the word is an 'imprecise term that conveys a precise image'.

Fulling Mill: To full is to increase the weight and bulk of cloth by shrinking, beating, pressing and washing. These processes were carried out at a fulling mill. Driven by water power, the mill replaced human feet in the process of fulling cloth. Mechanical hammers were linked by a system of cogs to a revolving waterwheel, alternately beating the length of cloth in a vat of water until it was felted evenly. The cloth was then stretched on racks.

Hide: In Domesday Book's entries of Chippenham Hundred, it has not been possible to define the amount of land it represents. It may be a fiscal measurement. *Carucate* has the same meaning.

Hundred: A division of a shire, created probably in the 10th century for tax and legal purposes.

Inn: (17th century) A hostelry for travellers, also selling wine to local inhabitants.

Laen: Derived from *loan*, hence an accurage description to apply to tenurial land in Saxon times.

Manor: The area over which a lord had domain in medieval times, later an estate with a dwelling house.

Messuage: A house with outbuildings.

Pottle: A measure of half a gallon, or a two-quart tankard or pot.

Press: A type of wardrobe for storing clothes in a bedchamber.

Probate inventories: A list of goods belonging to a deceased person. Before an estate could be settled, an inventory for probate was made by a reputable person. All goods and chattels had to be declared.

Tavern: (17th century) Essentially a wine shop, but food and drink were sold for consumption on the premises in some instances.

Villein: Highest level of peasantry at the time of the Domesday Survey.

Virgate: Like hide, difficult to define. There is some reason to believe in Wiltshire that it may have represented 30 acres.

Wainscot Chairs: *Wainscot* describes the panelling of a lower half of a wall; hence wainscot chairs were so called as they were designed to stand against a wall; therefore their backs lacked any design or decoration.

Bibliography

To read a list of all the sources consulted for this book is to ask too much of any reader. Those listed below were the most frequently used and have not been referred to in the text. If requested, the author will be glad to give any specific reference or source on any material in this book.

General

Barley, M. W., *English Farmhouse and Cottage* (1961).
Beresford, M., & Hurst, J. G., *Deserted Medieval Villages* (1972).
Blair, P. H., *Introduction to Anglo-Saxon England* (1977).
Blatcher, M., *Seymour Papers 1532-1686* (1968).
Bourne, J., *History of the Great Western Railway* (1846, repr. 1969).
Caird, J., *English Agriculture 1850-51* (1852).
Coleman, T., *Railway Navvies* (1968).
Copley, G., *Conquest of Wessex in the Sixth Century* (1954).
Denham, D. R., *Origins of Ownership* (1958).
Evans, J. G., *Environment of Early Man in the British Isles* (1975).
Finn, R. W., *Domesday Book: A Guide* (1973).
Gasquet, F. A., *Great Pestilence* (1893).
London Standing Conference for Local History. *Hedges and Local History* (1971).
MacDermott, E. T., *History of the Great Western Railway* (1927).
Mingay, G. E., *Rural Life in Victorian England* (1977).
Plomer, W., ed., *Kilvert's Diaries* (1961).
Postan, M. M., *Medieval Economy and Society* (1976).
Rham, W. L., *Dictionary of the Farm* (1850).
Richardson, J., *Local Historian's Encyclopedia* (1974).
Sawyer, P. H., ed., *Medieval Economy and Society* (1976).
Stenton, F. M., *Anglo-Saxon England* (1971).
Taylor, C., *Fields in the English Landscape* (1975).
Thirsk, J., ed., *Agrarian History of England and Wales* v. 1, 4, 8.
Titow, J. Z., *English Rural Society 1200-1350* (1969).
Whitelock, D., ed., *English Historical Documents* v. 1 (1979).
Youings, J., *Dissolution of the Monasteries* (1971).
Ziegler, P., *Black Death* (1969).

Local

Bettey, J. H., *Rural Life in Wessex* (1977).
Barron, R. S., *Geology of Wiltshire* (1976).
Chamberlain, J. A., *Chippenham* (1976).
Finsberg, H. P. R., *Early Charters of Wessex* (1964).
Goldney, F. H., *Records of Chippenham* (1889).
English Place Name Society, v. 16, *Place Names of Wiltshire* (1939).
LeLeux, S. A., *Brotherhoods Engineers* (1965).
Mann, J. de L., *Cloth Industry in the West of England 1640-1880)* (1971).
Ramsey, G. D., *Wiltshire Woollen Industry* (1943).
Rogers, K. H., *Wiltshire and Somerset Woollen Mills* (1976).
Tanner, G., *Calne Line* (1972).
Victoria History of Wiltshire, v. 1-5.
Walker, F., *Bristol Region* (1972).
Directories of Chippenham

Published Manuscripts

Cunnington, B. H., *Quarter Sessions Great Rolls for the Seventeenth Century* (1932).
Dugdale, W., *Monasticon Anglicanum* (1846).
National records published by the Public Record Office.
Pipe Roll Society publications.
Wiltshire Records Society, v. 1, 8, 10, 11, 13, 16, 26, 29.

Unpublished Manuscripts

In Chippenham Town Records
Documents pertaining to Cocklebury and Monkton.
The Municipal Records.

At the Library, Longleat House, Warminster
Seymour Papers relating to Monkton manor, especially v. 12, 127-32.

At the Wiltshire Archaeological Society Library, Devizes
Farmer's Notes by Eric Little.
William Gaby, His Book.
Vyner, B. E., Some Aspects of the Roman Settlement of Wiltshire North of the Chalk (1973 unpublished thesis).

At the Wiltshire Record Office
Ashe Family Documents.
Goldney Family Documents.
Deeds relating to Cocklebury and Monkton.
Maps of Proposed Locations of GWR and Calne railway lines.
Wills in Probate Registry.

Journals
Wiltshire Archaeological Magazine. Especially v. 15, 20, 49, 55, 56, 57.
Wiltshire Notes and Queries, v. 1-4.

Maps
Geological Survey of Great Britain Sheets 251, 266, 281.
Ordnance Survey of Great Britain, 7th Series, Sheets 173, 183, 184.

APPENDIX A

Borel ten̄ de .E. *Langefel* . Vluui tenuit T.R.E.7 geldb̄ p̄. vii.
hid . T̄ra . ē . vi . car̄ . De ea sꝼ in dn̄io . ii . hidæ . 7 ibi . ii . car̄ .
7 ii . ferui . 7 iiii . uilli 7 ix . cotar . 7 vii . cofcez . cū . iii . car̄ .
Ibi . viii . ac̄ p̄ti . 7 vi . ac̄ filuæ . Valuit . xl . fol . modo . iiii . lib̄ .
Idem Vluui ten̄ de ead̄ · tra . i . hid̄ . Valet . x . folid̄ .

Burghelm holds LANGLEY (Burrell) from Edward. Wulfwy held
it before 1066; it paid tax for 7 hides. Land for 6 ploughs,
of which 2 hides are in lordship; 2 ploughs there; 2 slaves;
  4 villagers, 9 cottagers and 7 Cottagers with 3 ploughs.
  Meadow, 8 acres; woodland, 6 acres.
The value was 40s; now £4.
  Wulfwy also holds 1 hide of this land; value 10s.

R̄ex ten̄ *Chepehā* . Rex . E . tenuit . Non geldauit . nec
hidata fuit . T̄ra . ē . c . car̄ . In dn̄io funt . xvi . car̄ . 7 xxviii .
ferui . Ibi . xlviii . uilli 7 xlv . bord 7 xx . cot . 7 xxiii . porcarij
Int om̄s hn̄t . lxvi . car̄ . Ibi . xii . molini de . vi . lib̄ . 7 c . ac̄
p̄ti . Silua . iiii . leu In lḡ 7 lat̄ . Paftura . ii . leu lḡ . 7 una leu
lat̄ . Hoc m̄ cū append fuis redd̄ firmā uni̅ noc̄tis cū om̄ib₅
c̄fuetudinib₅ 7 ual . cx . lib̄ ad numerū .
Huj̄ m̄ eccłam cū . ii . hid̄ ten̄ Ofb̄n ep̄s ex T.R.E . Vna ex his
hid̄ ē tainlande . altera ptin̄ æcclæ . Tot̄ ual . lv . folid̄ .
Huic m̄ ptin̄ una tra quā rex .E. dederat Vluiet uenatori
fuo . 7 erat de dn̄io fuo . H̄ in firma regis . ē m̄ . 7 p una hida habet̄
T̄ra . ē . ii . car̄ . 7 ipfæ ibi fꝼ . 7 iii . ferui . 7 iiii . uilli 7 iiii . cozets
cū . i . car̄ . Paftura . iiii . q̄₅ lḡ . 7 una q̄₅ lat̄ . Vat̄ . iii . lib̄ .
In firma huj̄ m̄ . ē dimid̄ v træ quæ fuit tainlande .
Edricus tenuit T.R.E

CHIPPENHAM. King Edward held it. It did not pay tax, and was
not assessed in hides. Land for 100 ploughs.
In lordship 16 ploughs; 28 slaves.
  48 villagers, 45 smallholders, 20 cottagers and 23 pigmen;
    between them they have 66 ploughs.
  12 mills at £6; meadow, 100 acres; woodland 4 leagues in
    length and width; pasture 2 leagues long and 1 league wide.
This manor with its dependencies pays one night's revenue,
with all customary dues.
Value £110 at face value.
  Bishop Osbern holds the church of this manor, with 2 hides,
since before 1066. One of these hides is thaneland; the other
belongs to the church. Total value 55s.
  To this manor belongs one land which King Edward gave
to Wulfgeat his Huntsman; and it was of his lordship; now
it is in the King's revenue and is recorded as 1 hide.
Land for 2 ploughs; they are there; 3 slaves;
  4 villagers and 4 Cottagers with 1 plough.
  Pasture 4 furlongs long and 1 furlong wide. Value £3.
In this manor's revenue is ½ virgate of land which was thaneland.
Edric held it before 1066.

Extracts from Domesday Book: Vol. 6, Wiltshire, *edited by*
Frank and Caroline Thorn (general editor John Morris)
Chichester 1979

Index

List of Subscribers

Florence Andrews
John D. Arnn
J. R. Ashford
Bernice M. Austin (Miss)
Jane H. Barnes
Michael J. Beacham
Mrs. Joan Stopford Beale
Pat and Bess Bilks
Marcia Blackman
Donald Box
John Brocklehurst
C. J. Rom Colthoff
Gloria Cook
Cooper-Wallis
Joyce, Lady Crossley
A. J. Dann
Mr. & Mrs. David Dickinson
Mr. & Mrs. Michael Dickinson
Norma and Joe Dunn
Anne Eddolls
Mrs. Bertram Ede
Paul Ensor
Kaye M. Fillmore
Rachel Latta Franck
Linda Frenkel
A. J. Funnell
Michael Gee
Bryan and Peggy George
Margaret Glide
D. and M. Gompels
Terence John Griffiths, MISTC
D. M. Hale, MRCVS
A. J. Hall
William S. Handley
Robert Harding
Anthony Harris
George Harris
Joan Harris
R. B. Harvey
Janette Hazell
Frank Heath
David A. Heinlein
R. B. Hillman

J. R. Hilton
Mrs. Jean P. Hitchman
Alan Hobbs
Mrs. P. M. Hodgson
Mrs. Gwen Hughes
Mr. & Mrs. L. H. Hughes
Mr. & Mrs. R. G. Hughes
William and Jayme Huleatt
Joy Hutchinson
G. B. Jamieson
Beatrice and Francis Johns
Edith S. Johnson
Edmond Johnstone
Hon. Mrs. D. O. Joly
E. Jones
Leonard Jones
Mrs. Else Kirkaldy
John and Barbara Kirkaldy
Richard Koprowski
Philip Lines
Jay Longan
Cllr. Maureen Frances Lloyd
Philip and Camilla Miles
Enid and Gillian Minter
Audley Money-Kyrle
Monkton Park School
M. G. Newbury
Bruce and Molly Newling
Dr. Robert A. Niederman
North Wiltshire District Council
P. V. Parton
Mrs. M. J. Phillips
Gabriel Pickar, MD
Robert Race
D. W. and M. R. Ragbourne
Peter Raphael
D. and M. J. Regan
Alan A. Richardson
G. H. and S. Ritchens
Robbiani
Mrs. D. M. Roddham
Barbara Rogers
S. F. Rooke

Lucy and Alexander Rostron
Robert L. Ruggiero
Enrique and Phyllis Santamarina
Leonard and Alice Santamarina
Richard Schwarz
Rebecca Ann Sederbaum
Gordon E. W. Self
Sheldon Manor
Sheldon School
Nat and Nina Shoehalter
Virginia Silver
G. E. Simpkins
Iris Bland Smith
June M. Smith
John A. Snyder
Mary and Morris Solotorovsky
Harry F. Stark
Beverly and Elliot Stempel
Margaret R. Stewart
Sheila F. Stewart
Robert Strunsky
Mrs. Thomas Suharik
Audrey Tickner
Mr. & Mrs. P. Q. Treloar
Bob and Warren Turner
S. W. Twine
The Tyrpien family
Ursula
J. Wakefield
Donald Watts
Mrs. Joy Weston
Miss E. M. Wheeler
Anthony White
Elizabeth Whiteway
Brian Wicks
Mary M. Williamson
Professor James R. Wilson
W. G. J. Wilson
Wiltshire County Council
Wiltshire, Folk Life Society
A. Wood
Spencer S. Zeigen

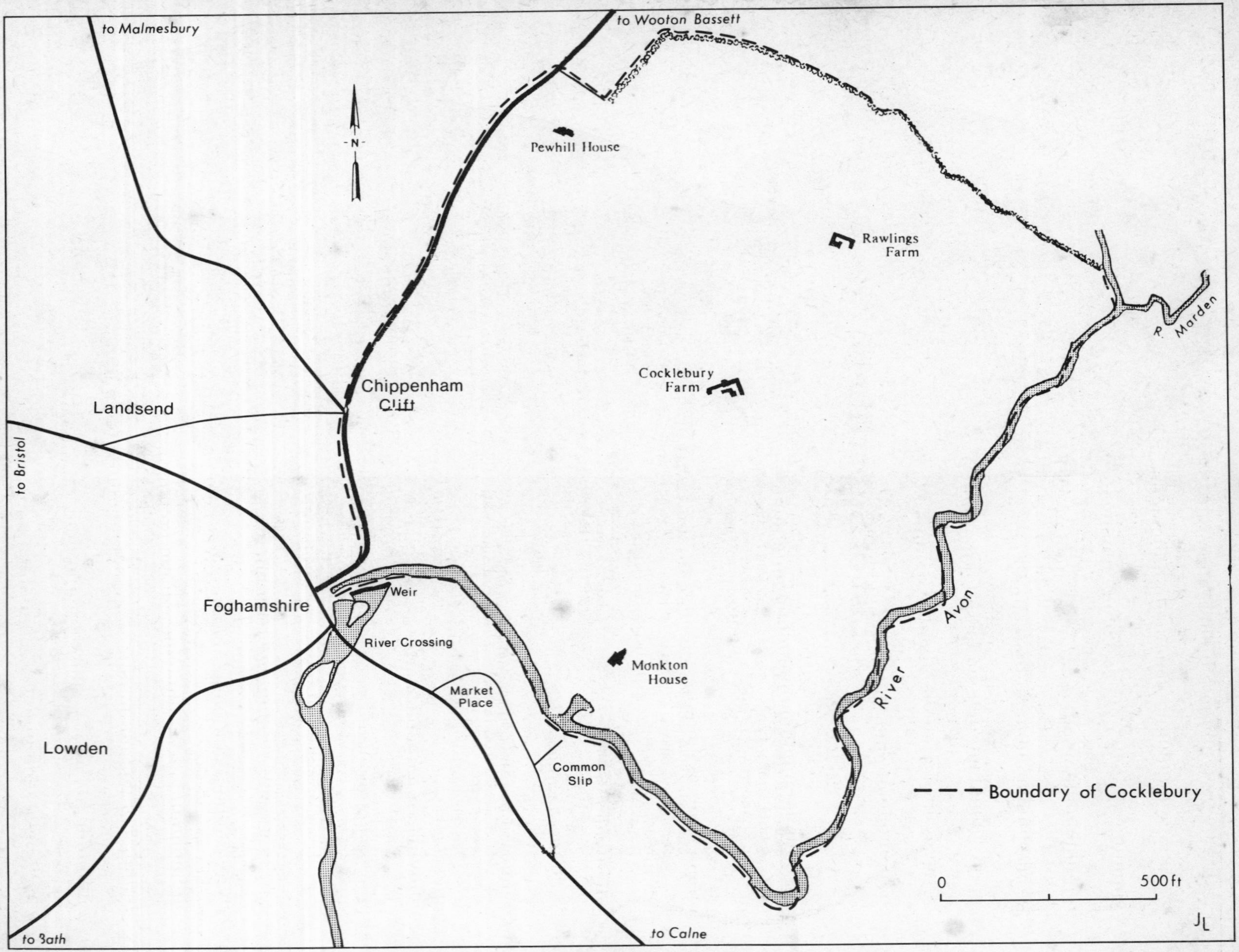

to Malmesbury

to Wooton Bassett

R Marden

Rawlings Farm

Cocklebury Farm

Pewhill House

Chippenham Cliff

Landsend

to Bristol

Foghamshire

Lowden

to Bath

Weir

River Crossing

Market Place

Common Slip

Monkton House

River Avon

to Calne

Cocklebury

N

– – – Boundary of Cocklebury

0   500 ft

J_L